Philosophy 101 by Socrates

Philosophy 101 by Socrates

An Introduction to Philosophy
via Plato's *Apology*

(Forty Things Philosophy Is
according to History's First
and Wisest Philosopher)

By Peter Kreeft

ST. AUGUSTINE'S PRESS
South Bend, Indiana

Manufactured in the United States of America

3 4 5 6 7   24 23 22

Library of Congress Control Number: 2014936437

∞ The paper used in this publication meets the minimum requirements of
the American National Standard for Information Sciences Permanence of
Paper for Printed Materials, ANSI Z39.481984.

The author expresses his appreciation for permission to reprint excerpts from
The Prince, translated with an introduction by George Bull
(Harmondsworth, England, and New York: Penguin Books, 1975);
The Prince: with Selections from *The Discourses*, translated by Daniel
Donno, edited and with an introduction by the translator
(Toronto and New York: Bantam Classic, 1981); and
Machiavelli, Selected Political Writings, translated by David Wootton
(Indianapolis: Hackett Publishing, 1994.) Reprinted by
permission of Hackett Publishing Company, Inc. All rights reserved.

ST. AUGUSTINE'S PRESS
www.staugustine.net

Contents

An Introduction to Socrates

There are three great introductions to philosophy that were written by three great ancient philosophers: the *Apology of Socrates*, by Plato, the *Protreptikos*, by Aristotle, and the *Hortensius*, by Cicero. Only the *Apology* has survived.

I should call them "matchmakers" rather than "introductions", because the purpose of all three of these little ancient classics is to have the beginners actually begin, not just *understand* philosophy but *do* it. St. Augustine says, in his *Confessions*, that Cicero's *Hortensius* did exactly that for him and changed his whole life.

This is this book's purpose too.

I have taught all levels of philosophy to all kinds of students for forty years, and I have never found a more effective way to accomplish that purpose (the intellectual seduction by which the student becomes a lover of wisdom, that is, a philosopher) than to begin with Socrates, especially the *Apology*. Thus this book: a portable classroom.

Reading Socrates is not like looking at a picture of a dead man; it is more like conversing with his ghost. For if you read any great book actively, especially if the book is in dialogue form, as Plato's are, you find it talking to you: asking you questions and demanding answers and answering your questions if you

7

actually ask them. It draws you in, into its activity of questioning. Like a ghost, it is almost alive.

When we read Plato's Socratic dialogues, it is almost like having the "Father of Philosophy" himself present as your teacher. It is the equivalent in philosophy to "practicing the presence of Christ" in Christianity or "being a Buddha" in Buddhism. The presence is very different in the three cases, but whatever it is, it is more than reading a book, though reading a book can be its catalyst. Remember, these three men, surely the three most influential teachers in history, together wrote—how many pages? Zero.

The dialogues of Socrates are the best introduction to philosophy because we learn any art best by apprenticeship to a great master, and no master of the art of philosophizing has ever been more simple, clear, and accessible to beginners than Socrates.

An Introduction to Philosophy

A sage is a lover of wisdom. A saint is a lover of God and man.[1] Being a sage is the second best thing we could possibly be, next to being a saint. "Philosophy" means "the love of wisdom" or "friendship" (*philia*) with wisdom (*sophia*). That is the essence of philosophy, that is its correct definition, that is what its inventor designed it to be.

For Socrates to "profess" to be a philosopher was not to be a university "professor". It was not to be a "professional" at all but an "amateur". "Amateur" means "lover". A philosopher loves wisdom; a "professional" loves money. Most philosophy professors today are professional employees of universities that hire them to sell their wisdom for money. Socrates would call them intellectual prostitutes. I am one of them. Boston College is my pimp.

But I am also a lover of wisdom, a philosopher; and philosophy is not intellectual prostitution but true

---

[1] "Man" means "mankind", not "males". It is traditional inclusive language. "Humanity" does not go with "God" ("God and humanity") because "God" and "man" are concrete nouns, like "dog" and "cat", while "divinity" and "humanity" are abstract nouns, like "canininity" and "felinity" or "dogginess" and "cattiness". Whatever the political or psychological uses or misuses of these words, that is what they mean. We do not undo old injustices against women by doing new injustices against language.

love because it loves truth. It loves a certain kind of truth called "wisdom".

Wisdom is more than knowledge. Knowing all the facts in a library does not make you wise. Wisdom is a knowledge not just of facts but of values, of what is humanly important; and it is a knowledge that is *lived*, that is learned by experience and lived out in experience.

Knowledge, like religion, is common. Wisdom, like saintliness, is rare.

An Introduction to This Book

This book is designed both for college classrooms and for "do-it-yourself" readers. It is designed both for introducing philosophy in general and for introducing Socrates in particular. And it is designed both for beginners in philosophy and for those who want to specialize in ancient Greek philosophy, especially Socrates.

It is not a book of technical textual or historical scholarship *about* Socrates and the origin of philosophy, but *an act of philosophizing*. It plays the same game Plato was playing in the *Apology*, but on a "little league" field: same game, lower level. It does not treat the *Apology* as a quaint, arcane, extinct bit of primitive data for some superior modern science to explain (or to explain away), but as a living example to imitate, a model partner with which to dialogue. In short, it tries to do the same thing Socrates did (philosophizing) rather than *explain* it or do something else, however valuable, such as scholarship *about* it.

There are many other aspects of the *Apology*—historical, psychological, political, textual—and many other good approaches to it. But this book uses it just to introduce philosophy.

I

The *Apology of Socrates*: Philosophy Defended

(*Forty Things Philosophy Is*)

1. ignorant (17a)
2. selfish (17a)
3. ironic (17a)
4. plain (17c)
5. misunderstood (18b)
6. a failure (8b–d)
7. poor (19e)
8. unscientific (19c)
9. unteachable (19e)
10. foolish (20e–23a)
11. abnormal (19c)
12. divine trickery (19e–20e)
13. egalitarian (22a)
14. a divine calling (22b)
15. laborious (22b)
16. countercultural (22a–e)
17. uncomfortable (24c)
18. virtuous (25c–26b)
19. dangerous (27e)
20. simplistic (28a)
21. polemical (28de)
22. therapeutic (29a)
23. "conformist" (29d)
24. embarrassing (29d–30a)

25. invulnerable (30c)
26. annoying (30e–31a)
27. pneumatic (31cd)
28. apolitical (31a)
29. docile (teachable) (33b)
30. messianic (33e)
31. pious (35d)
32. impractical (36bc)
33. happy (36e)
34. necessary (37de)
35. death-defying (39ab)
36. fallible (40c–41a)
37. immortal (41b)
38. confident (41d)
39. painful (41e)
40. agnostic (41e)

1. Philosophy is ignorant

The first words of the first sentence in Greek are: **"I do not know"** (*ouk oida*). This is the hidden key to the central meaning of the dialogue.[1] Plato usually gives the reader such a clue, to help him, and hides it, to test him. For example, the first words of the *Republic*, **"I went down to the Piraeus"**, signals Plato's descent into the "cave" of politics. The first words of the *Meno*, **"Can you tell me, Socrates"**, signals the point of the dialogue as the Socratic method of teaching by questioning, not by "telling". The first words of the *Phaedo*, **"Were you there with**

---

[1] Actually the *Apology* is one of the only two of Plato's thirty dialogues that is not, literally, a dialogue but a monologue, a speech—though it contains a little dialogue in which Socrates is allowed to cross-examine Meletos, one of his accusers.

Socrates?" ask the reader to identify with Socrates' life and death (Socrates dies in the *Phaedo*), somewhat as a Christian does with Christ's ("Were you there when they crucified my Lord? Were you there?"). The first words of the *Euthyphro*, **"This, Socrates, is something new?"** signals the fact that Socrates represents a fundamentally new kind of religion and piety that the old one (represented by Euthyphro) cannot comprehend.

The most unforgettable section of the whole *Apology*, for nearly all readers and for the subsequent history of philosophy, is the account of the Delphic oracle's pronouncement, relayed by Socrates' friend Chairophon, that no one in the world was wiser than Socrates, and Socrates' response: devoting his life to unraveling this riddle by trying to find someone wiser than himself, developing the "Socratic method" of cross-examination in order to do this, and concluding, now at his life's end, that he has solved the oracle's riddle. His solution: Though he has no wisdom at all (only God *has* wisdom, he says; man *pursues* it), this *is* wisdom—to know that he does not know—and the world must learn it if it wants to be wise. This is Lesson One, the first and most indispensable lesson. If we forget it, all subsequent lessons are only apparently learned.

Pascal said there are only two kinds of people: saints, who know they are sinners, and sinners, who think they are saints. He learned this wisdom, of course, from Jesus, who taught Socrates' Lesson One in religion. For Socrates would also say that there are only two kinds of people: the wise, who know they are fools, and fools, who think they are wise. In philosophy as in religion, pride is the deadliest sin.

So Socrates begins his defense, of himself as a philosopher and of philosophy itself, with his chief claim to fame, Lesson One—like the Zen master whose first lesson to the student eager to learn his wisdom is to pour tea into the student's cup until it overflows, and overflows more. "Master! Stop pouring! The cup is full." "Like your mind. How can I fill your cup if it is not empty?"

2. *Philosophy is selfish*

"*I almost forgot who I was.*" Philosophy is not *morally* selfish but *mentally* selfish. "Know thyself" (*gnothi seauton*) is almost philosophy's definition. You can be *knowledgeable* without knowing yourself, but you cannot be *wise* without knowing yourself. For if you do not know yourself, if you are a stranger to yourself. If you have never wondered about the knower, only about the known, then no matter how much knowledge you have, you do not know who has it.

"Know thyself" was inscribed over the Delphic oracle's temple. It was the first commandment of the god Apollo, who supposedly inspired the oracle (the "Sibyl", a prophetess who spoke in the god's name). The second was "nothing in excess". These two commandments summed up the wisdom of Apollo.

As we shall soon see, Socrates took these commandments, especially the first, more seriously than any other Athenian did. It was supremely ironic that he was the only Athenian ever executed for a religious crime.

Socrates' predecessors had wondered about many things—the elements, the heavenly bodies, the mysteries of nature, the gods, numbers—but Socrates philosophized only about human life and its moral problems—virtues and vices, wisdom and follies, rights and wrongs. Perhaps that was the reason he knew "Lesson One" so well: Nothing is harder to know than the self. No questions resist certainty and closure more than moral questions because nothing is deeper and closer to us. Try to measure the earth, and you may succeed (as one ancient Greek, Eratosthenes, actually did), and you may think you are wise; but try to measure yourself and your life's meaning and things like truth, goodness, and beauty, and you will find that you are swimming in waters far over your head. The world in your head is much bigger than the world outside your head.

Perhaps "know thyself" is not just difficult but impossible. Perhaps it is a *koan* (as Zen Buddhists would call it), an unsolvable puzzle that nevertheless teaches you and transforms your thought radically by its very unsolvability. For there always remains an "I" behind the "me", a knower behind the known, a subject behind the object, like the projecting machine behind the movie. How could what is not an object but the knowing subject ever become an object of knowledge?

I frankly doubt whether this is what Socrates meant by emphasizing "know thyself". It seems too modern, too subjective, too psychological. The ancients were like precocious children endlessly asking "What's that?" in a more objective way. Socrates probably meant by "know thyself", not "objectify the subject" or "define the indefinable unique individual you", but simply "know what it is to be a human being. Know the differences between men and beasts, between men and gods, and between good and evil."

This precious wisdom is what he ironically says he nearly forgot because his accusers were so persuasive. Their picture of him, as evil, corrupt and corrupting, dishonest and sophistic, impious and atheistic, was exactly the opposite of what he was; and he says their arguments for this false picture were so clever that they almost robbed him of his own self. No more precious property could possibly be at stake.

3. Philosophy is ironic

How you felt, gentlemen of Athens, when you heard my accusers, I do not know; but I—well, I nearly forgot who I was, they were so persuasive. Yet as for truth—one might almost say they have spoken not one word of truth. But what most astonished me in the many lies they told was when they warned you to take good care not to be deceived by me, "because I was a terribly clever speaker." They ought to have been ashamed to say it, because I shall prove them wrong at once by facts when I begin to speak, and you will see that I am not a bit of a clever speaker. That seemed to me the most shameless thing about them, unless of course they call one who speaks the truth a clever speaker. If that is what they mean, I would agree that I am not an orator of their class.

This is, of course, ironic. Irony is the contrast between appearance and reality, between what *seems* and what *is*, or between what we expect and what we discover.

Ancient Greek drama is full of irony, especially in

Sophocles. The Greeks became the world's greatest philosophers partly because they were ironic; they learned to question appearances to find something more, some hidden reality behind the appearances. Animals cannot do this, but "live by appearances", Aristotle says.

Philosophy is the love of wisdom; wisdom is seeing beyond appearances; and irony is this contrast. Therefore, philosophy is naturally ironic.

The ironic contrast Socrates refers to in his first sentence is the contrast between who he really is and who his accusers say he is, and try to persuade the jury he is, and nearly persuade Socrates himself he is. (So he says, with sarcastic, ironic exaggeration.) Who he really is, is the best man anyone there had ever met (as Plato calls him in his epitaph in the very last line in the *Phaedo*); but his accusers are persuading the jury that he is the *worst* man they ever met, a "**corrupter of the young**". He is also in truth the most pious man in Athens, but they will persuade the jury that he is an atheist. The irony is complete.

"**Yet as for truth—one might almost say they have spoken not one word of truth.**" The contrast Socrates points to here is between objective truth and subjective belief, or opinion. Truth cannot be destroyed, but it can be hidden, by our own foolish prejudices or dark desires; and "persuasion" can lead minds to falsehood as well as to truth.

Socrates' accusers love success in persuasion; Socrates loves truth. He is fanatically, absolutely single-minded in being devoted to truth. You might even say that truth is Socrates' god. He would certainly understand Gandhi's saying "God is not in strength but in truth."

And he asks his judges, the jurors, to be similarly single-minded, as judges ought to be: **"Please consider only one thing"** (18a). One is reminded of Jesus' similarly single-minded advice to Martha: "Martha, Martha, you are anxious and troubled about many things; one thing is needful" (Lk 10:42). The "one thing" Socrates asks them to consider is justice, which is a kind of truth, truth about right and wrong: **"Please consider only one thing and attend carefully to that—whether my plea is just or not"** (18a).

When the guardians of justice judge the just Socrates to be unjust, we have a supreme irony, a most striking contrast between appearance and reality. And—further irony—what is on trial here is philosophy, the love of true wisdom and the art of questioning appearances to find truth. Darkness is judging light.

4. Philosophy is plain

[Y]ou shall hear from me the whole truth; not eloquence, gentlemen, like their own, decked out in fine words and phrases, not covered with ornaments; not at all—you shall hear things spoken anyhow in the words that first come. For I believe justice is in what I say.

The weapons of Socrates' enemies are not truths but tricks, rhetorical tricks. What is rhetoric?

Rhetoric is the art of persuasion by words. In ancient Athens, which did not have modern media technology, rhetoric was a tremendously powerful tool, for it was a power over other people, not just nature, and over their minds, not just their bodies. Since it is powerful, it is dangerous, but it is not intrinsically evil. If it serves truth, it is good; if it serves falsehood, it is evil. There are honest ways to persuade people (by appealing to objective evidence and logic) and also dishonest ways (by appealing to anything other than truth and goodness, for example, fear, force, prejudice, lust, greed, pride, and so on).

From the Middle Ages until the latter half of the twentieth century, most liberal arts schools taught courses in rhetoric. Many required it. It was deemed not only useful but honorable. But the word "rhetoric" today usually connotes the misuse rather than the use of persuasion, and this was beginning to be so in Socrates' day, too. Thus Socrates *contrasts* it to philosophy. Instead of rhetoric, Socrates uses simple, plain speech, ordinary language, because this is *clearer*, and clarity is the servant of truth.

Rhetoric has not disappeared today, nor has it weakened; it has just changed its forms. In the past, its form was mainly oratory, that is, speechmaking, either political or religious or legal. Today its most powerful tools are not words but images, in TV and movies. In the "image media", words are subordinate to images: when words are used they are suggestive "sound bites" that call up images. In modern communications this is vastly preferred to argument. Can you recall the last logical argument you heard in an advertisement? Advertising has spread its technique everywhere: products are sold by suggestion, not reason. (Advertising is really the world's oldest profession. It began in the Garden of Eden: "See that apple? You need that apple! Eat that apple! Be like God!")

Proof of the power of rhetoric (advertising) today is very simple: rhetoric controls money, and money controls power. If you want to find that invisible thing, power, find the visible money trail. And one of the surest and quickest ways to get rich in our society is to learn to lie to people about how much they need your product.

Socrates is such a terrible salesman that he cannot even "sell" the truth about himself and save his own life. He is not "clever". His speech is not "covered with ornaments". He simply speaks the truth, the whole truth, and nothing but the truth.

(For a much more profound investigation of rhetoric versus philosophy, read Plato's *Gorgias*.)

It is significant that Socrates is an old man (17c), near death. Death's approach has a wonderful power to clarify and simplify things. Rhetoric loses its power in the face of death. Death is the friend of truth. Dr. Johnson says that he knows of no thought that so wonderfully clarifies a man's mind as the thought that tomorrow morning he will be hanged.

5. *Philosophy is misunderstood*

Suppose you were on trial for theft. Would you begin your defense by arguing that you were not a terrorist, a drug dealer, or a pimp?

Why, then, does Socrates, who is on trial for two things, "not believing in the gods of the state and corrupting the young", begin by defending himself against four other charges that no one brought against him?

Because he is a good psychologist, and he knows that these "other charges", or "old charges" as he calls them, are really the ones that move his accusers' minds and hearts, though not their lips. They are the unconscious, unexamined prejudices against him. And he wants to examine them. For, as he famously says, **"Life without enquiry is not worth living"** (38a).

Prejudices always come from familiar stereotypes, and the four "old charges" against Socrates are descriptions of the philosophy of other, more familiar philosophers, the "pre-Socratic philosophers". Two of them describe the cosmological, or physical, philosophers (primitive scientists, one might call them, though that is somewhat oversimplified); the other two describe the Sophists, the new breed of philosophers that arose within Socrates' lifetime in Athens.

There are many parallels between these two groups of philosophers in ancient Athens and the two groups of philosophers today that are loosely called "modernists" and "postmodernists". The modernists, like the ancient pre-Socratic cosmological philosophers, are interested in physical science, tend toward materialism, and believe in objective truth and the power of reason to find it. The postmodernists, especially the "deconstructionists", like the ancient Sophists, are interested in human, ethical, and, above all, political questions, and they are skeptics and subjectivists who call reason a disguise for power. (There is nothing new under the sun. The Greeks invented just about every school of philosophy that would appear for the next two millennia.)

The four "old charges" that constitute Athens' misunderstanding of Socrates and of true philosophy (for both are on trial here) are:

1. He is "**a highbrow**", that is, an "egghead", "smart-aleck", or "know-it-all". (Today we call them "experts".)

2. He is "**brainy in skylore**", that is, an astrologer, with his eyes on the stars and his head in the clouds. (Many of the ancients thought the stars controlled everything on earth.)

3. He "**has investigated what is under the earth**", that is, he is an alchemist or at least a physicist, like most of the "pre-Socratic" philosophers, who tried to unravel the secrets of the physical world, especially by finding what everything was made of, "the one in the many", and why everything moved.

4. He "**makes the weaker argument the stronger**", that is, he is a lawyer, a Sophist. It is only half a joke: the Sophists taught the art of successful persuasion, for a high fee, so that you could win cases in court no matter how weak or unjust your case might be. The Sophists were hated even more in Athens than lawyers are in America (which has 4 percent of the world's population and 75 percent of the world's lawyers). "We can make the weakest argument the strongest" was probably a familiar advertisement of the Sophists.

The real Socrates does not fit any of these descriptions, for he does not fit into either of the two categories of philosophers. He was not interested in physical science, like the cosmological philosophers and today's "modernists"; and he was not a skeptic, a subjectivist, a relativist, or a cynic who reduced truth to political power, like the Sophists and today's "postmodernists". He was not an "expert", an astrologer, an alchemist, or a lawyer.

But these were the familiar categories people had for philosophers in Athens, and Socrates was stuffed into them. ("He's one of them.") Those stereotypes, like most stereotypes, are not even exaggerations or oversimplifications; they are simply wrong. Socrates is a new kind of philosopher: one who, without arrogance, is confident about the use of human reason to find objective truth (like the cosmological philosophers and unlike the Sophists) but who, like the Sophists, is interested only in the "humanities", not the physical sciences, and most especially in ethics.

Socrates is so new that he is bound to be misunderstood. No other philosopher in history has owed so little to his predecessors. The gap between Socrates and all his predecessors is far greater than the gap between any two of his successors. He seems to have entered mankind's "great conversation" from outside, as if from another planet, even while being quintessentially Greek, as Jesus was quintessentially Jewish.

So if any philosopher is bound to be misunderstood, it is Socrates. And Socrates is the quintessential philosopher; Socrates is pure philosophy personified. Thus it is philosophy itself that is bound to be misunderstood. In this, as in many other ways, Socrates is to philosophy what Jesus is to religion.

(By the way, after Socrates' death, nearly every school of ancient philosophy claimed to be the true successors and disciples of Socrates, somewhat as

every Christian church and sect claims to represent
the true disciples of Christ.)

6. *Philosophy is a failure*

Socrates will not succeed in winning his most crucial argument, the one that is literally a matter of life
and death for him. Even Socrates, the world's greatest teacher, is a failure.

So was Jesus, in the world's eyes. So was Buddha.
So was Confucius. Few of their contemporaries understood or believed any of them. Yet their central
teachings were not technical and complex, but very
upfront and straightforward. It did not require a
Ph.D. to see it. It required a Ph.D. to *miss* it.

Socrates' death shows the power of prejudice. Socrates cannot defend himself against the four "old
charges", the prejudices against him. They will kill
him, and he foresees this.

> **Indeed, I have had many accusers complain-
> ing to you, and for a long time, for many
> years now, and with not a word of truth to
> say; these I fear, rather than Anytos and his
> friends, although they, too, are dangerous;
> but the others are more dangerous, gentle-
> men, who got hold of most of you while you
> were boys, and persuaded you . . . at an age
> when you would be most likely to believe, . . .
> accusing in a case which goes by default, with
> no one to defend. The most unreasonable
> thing is that it is impossible to know their
> names. . . . For there is no possibility of hav-
> ing them produced here, or of cross-ques-**

tioning any one of them, but having to defend oneself against them is just like being compelled to fight with shadows, and cross-question with none answering. (18b–d)

The power of prejudice is darkness. It is not just ignorance but ignorance of your own ignorance. Prejudice is very easy to create and reinforce by rhetoric and advertising and images that bypass the reason; for that which bypasses reason works in the dark. Even the heavyweight champion of the world will lose to a flyweight if he has to fight blind. Even the world's greatest surgeon will be unable to perform the simplest operation if the lights go out in the operating room.

Socrates knows this. Even the world's greatest teacher, whose arguments are sharp and bright like swords, cannot fight against a fog. He will defend himself very well when he cross-examines Meletos, his accuser. (Athenian law required the man who brought legal charges against another to submit to cross-examination, and even to pay the fine or penalty that he sought from the defendant if he lost the case.) But Socrates cannot defend himself against "everyone" and no one. A prejudice is something "everybody" knows and "nobody" defends.

To philosophize is to demand light. All opinions must be examined. Terms must be clearly defined, reasons and evidence given, and assumptions exposed. This is not just logic; it is justice, fairness, and honesty. This is also the essential method of science as well as philosophy. (What we call the sciences were not sharply distinguished from philosophy until after Newton. Historically, most of the sciences were spin-offs from philosophy, like children who moved away from their parents' home and became independent.)

Each of the sciences is successful and popular because each science generates a practical application, a technology, that gives us more power over the material world and satisfies our material desires. But philosophy is unpopular, by its very nature, because it does not satisfy our material desires but questions them, and us, like a cross-examining lawyer.

7. *Philosophy is poor*

Socrates makes a point that he never took a fee for his teaching. (Neither did Jesus.) This proved that he was not one of the Sophists, who sold their minds as a prostitute sells her body.

There is another reason Socrates never made any money out of philosophy. He had nothing to sell. He claimed to *have* no wisdom, only to seek it.

The Sophists approached wealthy Athenians with this reasonable solicitation: "Our minds are full—full of clever rhetorical tricks to confuse juries—and our purses are empty. Your purses are full and your minds are empty. Let's make a mutually profitable exchange. Grease our palms with your silver, and we will oil your brains with our wisdom." Many wealthy Athenian parents were paying expensive tuition to Sophists to tutor their children without examining what product they were buying. Just change one word in that sentence—"Athenian" to "American"—and you see that "the more things change, the more they stay the same."

Socrates offered the opposite service from the

Sophists: to be the garbage man of his students' minds, to take *out* ideas rather than to put them in. What ideas? Follies, fallacies, fancies, fantasies, prejudices. You emerge from a conversation with Socrates poorer, not richer, in opinions.

What do we use money for? Ordinarily, money represents material goods or services that we want to exchange for others. For example, we pay $100,000 for heart surgery because health is worth more to us than two $50,000 luxury cars. But wisdom has no price because it is not a material good.

All material goods diminish when shared: you have less money, fame, power, and so forth, after you give some away. But wisdom, like love, multiplies when shared, because wisdom is not a material good.

Yet very many people pursue wealth as their most important end. If someone is suddenly happy, the most common comment from friends is "What happened to you? Did you win the lottery?" But money is only "a *means* of exchange", therefore, it cannot be the *end*, goal, purpose, meaning, or final good of human life.

If you should ever decide to study philosophy, someone is sure to ask you, "What can you do with it?" The answer is "Nothing. But it can do something with me."

8. *Philosophy is unscientific*

Philosophy is not *anti*-scientific, just *not*-scientific.

The kind of philosophy Socrates founded *is* a "science" in the broad, ancient sense of the word: an organized body of knowledge that explains things through their causes. But it is *not* a science in the modern sense of the word: it is not limited to "the scientific method" and to the empirically verifiable (that is, that which is provable by sense observation and experiment) and to the quantifiable, the mathematically measurable, which is the criterion for an exact or "hard" science.

Most of the thinking of most of the "pre-Socratic philosophers" (Thales, Anaximander, Anaximines, Heraclitus, Parmenides, Pythagoras, Empedocles, Anaxagoras, Democritus) was about the physical world and centered on the question: What is "the one" behind "the many"? What is everything made of? (The answers given were, respectively: water, "stuff", air, fire, "being", number, the four elements, "seeds", and atoms.)

Socrates, like the Sophists, simply was not interested in the questions of physical science, but only in moral questions. Obviously, moral questions (like "what is justice?") cannot be answered by the scientific method, because moral qualities are not visible (what color is justice?) or quantitatively measurable (how much does it weigh?). But that does not mean they cannot be settled by reason at all.

9. *Philosophy is unteachable*

So says (or implies) Socrates, the greatest teacher of it. He contrasts philosophers ("lovers of wisdom") with the Sophists (so-called "wise men") by noting that the Sophists claimed to teach the art of living, but *he* cannot teach this knowledge:

> **"Callias", I said, "if your two sons were colts or calves, we should know how to hire and**

pay a manager for them, to make them well-bred in the virtue proper to those animals; he would be a horse-trainer or a farmer; but now, since they are human beings, whom have you in mind to be their manager? Who is an expert in such virtue, human or political? . . . I . . . should give myself fine airs and graces if I had the knowledge. But I have not. (20a–c)

If wisdom were teachable, wise men like Pericles would have been able to teach it to their sons and make them wise. But Pericles could not. (Neither could Socrates!)

Socrates uses this argument in another dialogue, the *Meno*, to argue that virtue cannot be taught. He does this right after arguing that it *can* be taught because it is knowledge: We always seek what we think is good for us, so when we seek evil it must be because we think it will be good for us; we think it will make us happy. If we only *knew* that it is virtue that always makes us truly happy, we would always seek virtue and never vice.

Both arguments seem strong, yet they prove contradictory conclusions: that virtue cannot be taught, and that it can. Socrates' teaching does not tell us the answer. The first words of the *Meno*, **"Can you tell me, Socrates . . . ?"** indicate that the central point of that dialogue will be the contrast between *teaching* and *telling*; between Socrates' method of teaching by questioning and by inveigling us to ask the great, hard questions, and "telling", which was the Sophists' method of lecturing, telling us the answers they claimed to know.

Socrates believes that the most important questions are not "factual" questions, like what causes the tides, whose answers can be known and taught, but "value" questions, like what justice is and why we should pursue it. And even though he strongly believes that the true answers to "value" questions, that is, moral questions, are just as objective as the true answers to "factual" questions, he does not claim to know and teach the answers to these questions, but only to help us to ask them, to make the journey ourselves.

We could almost say that according to Socrates, anything worth teaching cannot be taught, and anything teachable is hardly worth teaching. Philosophy, the pursuit of wisdom, cannot be *taught*. It can only be *shown* in action, by a lover of wisdom like Socrates. And only the process (the love), but not the result (wisdom), can be imitated. Philosophy cannot be *taught*, like math; it must be *caught*, like measles.

10. Philosophy is foolish

Socrates admits he has a certain kind of wisdom: **"perhaps the only wisdom that men can have"**. It is the wisdom that knows its own foolishness. For only God *possesses* wisdom, or *is* wise (23a), while man *pursues* it, loves it, courts it. This is why Socrates claims the name "philosopher" ("lover of wisdom"), and not "Sophist" ("wise man"). It is a confession of humility rather than a claim of pride.

These two things naturally go together: belief in God and humility. These two things also naturally go together: skepticism about God and pride. For if there is no God, then man is the highest and wisest of all beings. But if there is a God or gods, then human wisdom, now judged by a higher standard, is relatively tiny. However proud and arrogant some religious *believers* may have been, humility is inherent in the very logic of religious *belief.* And however humble some unbelievers may have been, lack of humility is inherent in the very logic of unbelief.

No one saw this connection between humility (before truth) and belief (in God) more clearly than philosophy's most passionate atheist, Nietzsche. If there is no God, no eternal mind, he reasoned, then there is no eternal truth. Truth is only God without a face. Nietzsche dared to ask "the most dangerous question . . . why truth? Why not rather untruth?" Why indeed? Dostoyevski also pursued this dangerous question through some of his characters (Ivan Karamazov, Stavrogin, Raskolnikov): "If there is no God, then everything is permissible." Once this connection is seen, we can either run into the abyss of darkness by embracing both the "if" and the "then", or run into the abyss of light by denying both and embracing God, eternal truth, and objective goodness.

But should we not give reasons for this momentous choice? But how can we, since it is reason and truth themselves that are in question?

Socrates never visited these terrifying heights and depths; they are distinctively modern and post-Christian. Socrates was a simple virgin; Christians are like married women (married to God), and modernists are like divorcees. He is too young for divine wisdom; modernists are too old.

11. *Philosophy is abnormal*

Paradoxically, what gets Socrates into trouble is his humility. By ordinary standards he is fanatically humble, immoderately moderate, and immodestly modest. And this implicitly insults the rest of the world, showing it up as proud and foolish.

After claiming he has no knowledge to teach, he says,

> **Some one of you then might . . . ask perhaps, "Well, Socrates, what is your business? Where did these calumnies come from? For all this talk about you, and such a reputation, has not arisen, I presume, when you were working at nothing more unusual than others do; it must be you were doing something different from most people." (20c)**

To philosophize is not to accept normalcy, to be dissatisfied with the normal and with normal "wisdom", to seek a higher wisdom, and perhaps not to find it. But the very search puts "normal" into question.

12. *Philosophy is divine trickery*

The passage about "the god" of the Delphic oracle is the most memorable in the whole *Apology*. Thirty years from now, when someone asks you whether you have ever read the *Apology*, this is the passage you will remember.

It begins when Socrates calls in a character witness to support his defense against the charge of atheism: the character witness is a god! **"What I am going to tell you is not my word, but I will refer it to a speaker of sufficient authority: I will call the god in Delphi as witness of my wisdom"** (20e). Not directly, of course, but through a chain of witnesses: we, like the Athenians, receive from Socrates what Socrates received from his friend Chairophon's brother, who received it from Chairophon, now deceased, who received it from the priests of the oracle, who received it from the Sibyl, the prophetess-oracle, who supposedly received it from the god himself (Apollo). Religion always involves faith, a faith in the intermediaries, thus faith in humans, as well as in God.

When Socrates says that **"What I am going to tell you is not my word, but . . . a** [higher] **authority"**, note the similarity to Jesus' claim to speak only the word he had received from his Father (Jn 14:24). And when Socrates refers to this chain of witnesses, note the similarity to the claim of the Church to pass down the links of time's chain what she originally received from Jesus (Lk 10:16).

One can imagine the day Socrates received the god's disturbing word from his friend Chairophon, who had just returned from pilgrimage to Delphi:

"Socrates, Socrates! I got to ask the god a question! I waited for days, and then I got lucky! I conversed with the god!"

"You were allowed to ask just one question, right?"

"Right."

"So what did you ask? 'What is the meaning of life?' 'Will I go to heaven?' 'What is virtue?' 'Why do the Red Shoes team always lose the final game of the Olympics?' "

"No, Socrates, I asked whether there was anyone in the world who was wiser than Socrates."

"What? You fool, Chairophon! What an opportunity you missed! I could have answered that one; you didn't need a god. You may as well have asked him whether the sky is blue."

"Don't you want to hear the god's answer, Socrates?"

"No."

"That's right. No. That was his answer."

"You can't possibly mean—"

"I do. The god of Delphi said that there is no one in the world wiser than you, Socrates."

At this point Socrates probably dropped the stone he was cutting (he was a stonecutter) and broke his toe. He tells us what he thought: **"What in the world does the god mean? What in the world is his riddle? For I know in my conscience that I am not wise in anything, great or small; then what in the world does he mean when he says I am wisest? Surely he is not lying? For he must not lie"** (21b). (For he is a god.)

At this point Socrates has a crisis, a contradiction between his faith and his experience, his reason, and his conscience. A lesser man would either simply abandon his faith or abandon his reason, his conscience, or his experience. But Socrates, knowing that the oracle often speaks in puzzles and riddles, hoped to save both his faith and his reason by *exploring* the riddle. It would cost him a total change of life and career, from stonecutter to philosopher. Philosophy, in fact, was born that day. All philosophers should celebrate Chairophon Day as a holy day.

"I was puzzled for a long time to understand

what he meant; then I thought of a way to try to find out, something like this: I approached one of those who had the reputation of being wise" (21b). Socrates hoped to bring this wise man to the oracle and demand from the oracle an explanation of his riddle: **"Here is one wiser than I, but you said I was wiser."** Then, hopefully, the god would explain his riddle.

But Socrates never got to that point because he never found a wise man. What he found instead was the art of cross-examination that tested men's wisdom, the art that became the method of philosophy. The god tricked Socrates into becoming the world's first philosopher by his riddle. Instead of revealing it directly, instead of telling Socrates what to do, he used the Socratic method on Socrates, the method of planting a puzzle in a mind and watching it grow. The god was very tricky.

Once Socrates applied his method of questioning, he realized the truth of half of the god's riddle: that those who seemed wise were not. Later, he would understand the other half: that he, who was not wise but knew it, was in fact wise.

When I examined him, then—I need not tell his name, but it was one of our statesmen whom I was examining when I had this strange experience, gentlemen—and when I conversed with him, I thought this man seemed to be wise both to many others and especially to himself, but that he was not; and then I tried to show him that he thought he was wise, but was not. Because of that he disliked me ... but I went away thinking to

myself that I was wiser than this man; the fact is that neither of us knows anything beautiful and good, but he thinks he does know when he doesn't, and I don't know and don't think I do: so I am wiser than he is by only this trifle, that what I do not know I don't think I do. (21cd)

"This man" turned out to be typical man and "this trifle" (the word is ironic) is merely the first and most indispensable part of wisdom, the Lesson One without which there is no Lesson Two.

Socrates finally solved the riddle of the oracle. He is indeed the wisest of men, and he has no wisdom at all, and those two truths do not contradict each other, as they seem to, because of Lesson One.

The god of the oracle taught humanity to philosophize by this trick, this riddle. It is not just for Socrates. Through Socrates, his prophet, the god challenges all of mankind to begin the philosophical life, the quest for wisdom, by dividing all of mankind henceforth into disciples of Socrates and others; between those who have learned Lesson One and those who have not; between the wise, who know they are fools, and the fools, who think they are wise.

In fact, 2036 years later, modern philosophy began when René Descartes published the landmark *Discourse on Method* (essentially a plea to philosophers to imitate the newly successful scientific method), which began, in the very first sentence, by asserting the exact opposite of the Socratic wisdom summarized in the last sentence of the preceding paragraph. Descartes assumes, instead, that we all *are* wise and gives as his reason for believing this fact that we all *think* we are wise:

Good sense [wisdom] is the most evenly distributed commodity in the world, for each of us considers himself to be so well endowed therewith that even those who are the most difficult to please in all other matters are not wont to desire more of it than they have. It is not likely that anyone is mistaken about this fact. Rather, it provides evidence that the power of judging rightly and of distinguishing the true from the false (which, properly speaking, is what people call good sense or reason) is naturally equal in all men. Thus the diversity of opinions does not arise from the fact that some people are more reasonable than others, but simply from the fact that we conduct our thoughts along different lines [use different methods] and do not consider the same things [data].[2]

13. Philosophy is egalitarian

The claim that philosophy is egalitarian may seem to contradict our previous point of Socrates' superior wisdom and his division of humanity into two classes: the wise (who know they have no wisdom) and the foolish (who think they have it). To say philosophy is egalitarian seems to side with Descartes instead of Socrates.

---

[2] *Discourse on Method*, trans. Donald Cress (Indianapolis: Hackett Publishing, 1980), p. 1.

Yet Socrates himself interprets the oracle's riddle, that "there is no man wiser than Socrates", in an egalitarian way, as inviting all men equally to learn Lesson One and share Socrates' wisdom:

The truth really is, gentlemen, that the god in fact is wise, and in this oracle he means that human wisdom is worth little or nothing, and it appears that he does not say this of Socrates, but simply adds my name to take me as an example, as if he were to say that this one of you human beings is wisest, who like Socrates knows that he is in truth worth nothing as regards wisdom. (23ab).

Philosophy is egalitarian because it is the love of wisdom, which begins in Socrates' Lesson One, humility. "Humility" comes from *humus*, which means "earth" or "ground". Nothing is more egalitarian than earthiness. We all stand on this common ground: we are all humans, not gods, and judged by divine standards *all* "**human wisdom is worth little or nothing**", though by human standards some men seem very wise and considerably wiser than others. From a high mountaintop, all men look like ants; from the street level, some look taller than others.

14. Philosophy is a divine calling

Socrates is on trial for atheism. He will be executed because he seems to Athens to be guilty of "not believing in the gods the state believed in but in other gods instead". Socrates evidently did *not* believe in any of the gods officially approved by the state; for if he had, he could have saved his life simply by uttering one sentence: "I believe in _____ as the state believes", filling in the blank with any one of the approved gods. For Athens was a religious smorgasbord: you could choose any god you wished, and mere profession of faith was sufficient. But Socrates could not honestly do this. (A clever prosecutor could have shown this easily.)

And the reason Socrates did not believe in the gods of the state was because he philosophized. He questioned. Yet—the supreme irony of the trial—philosophy itself, that offensive enterprise that made his enemies fear and hate and kill him because they feared it led to atheism—is a divine vocation, a divine call, a divine command. Every single time Socrates mentions philosophy in the *Apology* he mentions its origin and pins it to "the god". Philosophizing is **"the god's way"** (22a); **"where God posted me . . . with the duty to be a philosopher"** (28e); **"help[ing] the god by proving that the man is not wise"** (23b); **"my service of the god"** (22e; 30a); **"something stuck on the state by the god"** (30e) ("stuck" like a fly on flypaper); **"commanded by the god"** (33c).

A similar irony attaches to Jesus. Even non-Christians, who do not believe he is God, almost always agree that he was a saint; but he was executed for irreligion, for blasphemy. Apparently a little piety is respectable and safe; serious, honest piety is so dangerous that it is often fatal.

15. Philosophy is laborious

Socrates calls his philosophical "wanderings" **"my own Labours"** (22a), referring to the well-known legend of the twelve labors of Hercules, the Greek

Superman. There are two surprises here: that a philosopher could compare himself with a superhero and that philosophy is laborious.

Which is a greater labor: to leap tall buildings in a single bound or to think seriously and honestly about the questions of philosophy? Who is the greater hero, Superman or Socrates? That depends on whether soul or body is more important.

Whether philosophy is easy, like watching a movie, or laborious, like childbirth, depends on whether you are only observing some other philosophers in action, passively, or actually philosophizing yourself, actively (either in dialogue with another or alone), and on whether you are honestly trying to find the truth or just pretending, whether you are actually thinking or just imagining that you are thinking. It is surprising how easy it is to deceive yourself into believing you have done it when you have only imagined doing it; for "it" is thinking, and imagining can easily be confused with thinking.

16. Philosophy is countercultural

Philosophy questions and challenges societies and cultures as well as individuals. It is always, therefore, somewhat "countercultural", for it neither thoughtlessly ignores the social and cultural dimension of life nor thoughtlessly conforms to culture. It questions the assumptions and values of whole societies and segments of society, just as it questions the assumptions and values of individuals.

In the *Apology* Socrates is required, by law, to address the society that is judging him. Unlike his most famous disciple, Plato, who wrote the world's most famous book of social and political philosophy, the *Republic*, Socrates did not go into politics, even in thought, but preferred to question individuals one at a time, throughout his life. But he mentions the social dimension of his one-by-one philosophizing here by dividing his life's Herculean "**Labours**" into dialogues with three social groups. He first questions statesmen, then poets and musicians, then craftsmen (21e–22e). Why does he mention these three groups?

Because they constituted the three most socially influential and respected groups in his culture. In ours, too, for they correspond to the masters of the social sciences (statesmen), the arts (poets), and the natural sciences and technology (craftsmen), though of course in a simple and primitive form. These are the three fundamental divisions of everything we think worth knowing and teaching in colleges and universities ("the arts and sciences"). So Socrates cross-examined his whole society, in order, in three basic parts.

And all three parts are out to "get" him. He has three accusers: Anytos, Meletos, and Lycon; and he notes that "**Meletos** [is] **angry on behalf of the poets, and Anytos for the craftsmen and statesmen, and Lycon for the orators**" (23e). (Orators, like the Sophists, were either poets or statesmen, or both, or learned from the poets and taught and served the statesmen.) The whole of society, the whole world, fails to understand Socrates and fears him. The whole world is equally guilty of his death.

Again there is a surprising similarity with Jesus. The charge against him, placed on the Cross, was written in Hebrew, in Latin, and in Greek. These were the three most important languages and cultures in the premodern Western world, the three that would give us today nearly everything we value from our past. The whole world also failed to understand Jesus and feared him (and his followers, the best of whom down through the centuries are repeatedly martyred). The whole world is equally guilty of his death, too. The two greatest teachers of wisdom to our culture, our culture's two most influential heroes, were both profoundly countercultural.

By the way, Socrates does not say that poets, statesmen, and craftsmen are worthless or know nothing; but that they do not *understand* what they say, that they have no *wisdom* (22e). The craftsmen, he found, knew **"much of real value"** and **"they knew what I did not"** (22d); but because they could manage this art well, each one claimed to be very wise in other things also, **"the greatest things"** (22d). Thus they, too, lacked Lesson One.

Neither politics nor art nor science nor technology can tell us what we are and what we should be, why we live and why we die, what is good and what is evil. These are the questions of a higher, harder enterprise: philosophy, the pursuit of wisdom. Wisdom rightly judges and challenges and rebukes politics, art, science, and technology. Whether Napoleon was a political success is a political question; whether he was a success as a human being is a philosophical question. Whether Wagner's music is beautiful is an artistic question; "What is beauty?" is a philosophical question. Whether "natural selection" happened is a scientific question; what its religious significance is is a philosophical question. Whether cloning humans is possible is a technological question; whether it is moral is a philosophical question.

17. *Philosophy is uncomfortable*

This is obvious from the little dialogue with Meletos. Would you be comfortable if you were Meletos and had to answer Socrates' cross-examination?

Philosophy says to us, as Socrates says to Meletos, **"Meletos, stand up here before me and answer."** The law compelled Meletos to do that; honesty also compels us. Philosophizing honestly sometimes feels like looking through a keyhole and finding an eye looking back at you.

Honest philosophy is uncomfortable because it judges us, or it makes us judge ourselves. Socrates, personifying philosophy, judges the man who would judge him: "[Meletos] **says I am a criminal, who corrupts the young. . . . But I say, gentlemen, that Meletos is a criminal who is making a jest of serious things by prosecuting people lightly, by pretending to be serious and to care for things which he has never cared about at all"** (24c). Socrates cares about the soul; Meletos does not. This is a serious matter, the care of souls. It requires wisdom. It is precious, but uncomfortable.

John Stuart Mill said, "It is better to be Socrates dissatisfied than a pig satisfied." What do you say?

18. *Philosophy is virtuous*

True philosophy, Socrates claims, will make you a better person. Philosophy is the key to virtue.

Not the *knowledge* of philosophy but philosophy, "the love of wisdom", will make you good. Obviously, mere knowledge, intelligence, cleverness, a Ph.D., and a high I.Q. do not make you good: some of the

most wicked people in history have been the smart-
est. Yet Socrates insists that "virtue is knowledge",
that "vice is ignorance", and that "no one does wrong
knowingly." He teaches this paradox in a number of
other dialogues and also here, in his cross-examination of Meletos (25c–26b). What kind of knowledge
and ignorance is he talking about?

Not a knowledge of facts, but a knowledge of values; in fact, an *understanding* of values and of the truth
that doing good is always personally profitable, that
virtue makes you happy, that "justice is always more
profitable than injustice" (the fundamental conclusion proved in the *Republic*). If the thief only knew,
that is, fully understood, that is, personally realized
(what Newman called "real assent") that filling his
pockets with stolen money would not make him
happy but filling his soul with virtue would, because
he *is* his soul, not his pockets—if he realized that, he
would not be a thief. If he only knew (with this deep
knowledge described above) that virtue was the path
to happiness, he would practice virtue, because all
men want happiness. Those who do not choose
virtue think that vice will make them happy. And this
thought is false; it shows a lack of knowledge, or
rather of wisdom. It fails to question appearances. If
sin did not *seem* like fun, we would all be saints.

Rarely does Socrates claim to know something, to
teach something, to give us answers. Usually he gives
us only questions and a method for *pursuing* answers.
The three "answers", or positive discoveries, or
"teachings", Socrates does give us are all paradoxes,
apparent contradictions to what seems obviously true
to common sense:

1. Virtue is knowledge; evil is ignorance; no one knowingly does evil. (*Apology, Meno, Protagoras*)

2. Learning is really remembering, recollection (*anamnēsis*). (*Meno, Phaedo*)

3. No evil can ever happen to a good man. (*Apology, Republic*)

Here is how the first paradox is argued for in the *Apology*, in Socrates' cross-examination of Meletos:

Is it better to live among good citizens or bad ones? . . . Don't the bad ones do some harm to those who are at any time nearest to them, and the good ones some good?

"Certainly."

Then is there anyone who wants to be damaged by his associates rather than to be helped? . . .

"No, certainly."

Very well. You bring me here as one who corrupts the young generation and makes them worse: Do you say that I mean to do it, or not?

"You mean to do it is what I say."

. . . Have I indeed come to such a depth of ignorance that I do not know even this—that if I make one of my associates bad I shall risk getting some evil from him—to such a depth [of ignorance] as to do so great an evil intentionally, as you say? . . . But if I do it without intent, there is no law to bring a man into court for accidental mistakes such as this; on the contrary, the law is that one should take

him apart privately and instruct and admonish him [this is what Socrates spent his life doing]: **for it is plain that, if I learn better, I shall stop what I do without intent. But you shirked meeting me and instructing me; you would not do that, and you bring me to this court, where it is the law to summon those who need punishment, not instruction.** (25c–26a)

Socrates seems to imply that *no* one needs punishment, only instruction, if all evildoing is involuntary and due to ignorance. Whether this is what he actually believed, or whether he is just provoking us to think for ourselves to refute his paradoxical teaching, is of interest to the historian, who is more concerned with Socrates, now dead, than with himself. But whether it is true or false, and why, and the consequences for one's own life, are of interest to any lover of wisdom.

And to society. For if Socrates is right here, then it is schools rather than prisons that are the answer to crime: schools that persuade their students that vice never profits and that harming others' bodies always harms your own soul and thus replace "outer cops" with "inner cops", that is, effective consciences.

But if Socrates is wrong, then he has failed to penetrate to the root cause of evil and, thus, also failed to provide its cure.

But he certainly is not wrong in provoking us to think, by his provocative paradox, about this crucial question. Jesus shocked us by praying, "Father, forgive them *for they know not what they do*", regarding his crucifiers; Socrates shocked us by saying the same thing regarding everybody.

19. *Philosophy is dangerous*

Philosophy always makes enemies, as sanctity also does. *All* the saints had enemies, controversies, and human conflicts. For when light meets darkness or when good meets evil there can be no reconciliation, no peace.

Thus Socrates notes that he "**was heartily disliked by many**" (28a). If you do not understand why a wise and good man like Socrates (or Jesus) is hated by many, you do not understand Socrates or Jesus or human nature or yourself. ("Know thyself" is *much* more difficult than you think!) If you are shocked or puzzled to hear that philosophy or sanctity is dangerous, you do not understand philosophy or sanctity or human nature or yourself.

Socrates, however, understands:

Well, gentlemen, I am no criminal according to Meletos's indictment; that needs no long defence from me to prove, but this is enough. However, when I said some time ago that I was heartily disliked by many, you may be sure that it is quite true. And this is what will convict me, if anything does, not Meletos or Anytos but the prejudice and dislike of so many people. The same thing has convicted many other good men, and I think will do so again; there is no fear it will stop with me. (28ab)

Socrates knew far less history than we but learned more from it. In fact his prophetic foresight is more accurate than many people's hindsight, many centuries later.

If we think we are automatically free from the danger of ignorant prejudice and tyranny simply because we are a democracy, we should reflect on the fact that it was a democracy that killed Socrates. A democracy can be as ignorant, as prejudiced (especially by fashion and popularity), and as tyrannical as a monarchy. There is no automatic connection between numbers (how many rule) and wisdom or virtue, between quantity and quality.

20. Philosophy is simplistic

But perhaps someone may say: Are you not ashamed then, Socrates, at having followed such a practice that you now run a risk of a sentence of death? I would answer such a one fairly: You are wrong, my friend, if you think a man with a spark of decency in him ought to calculate life or death; the only thing he ought to consider, if he does anything, is whether he does right or wrong, whether it is what a good man does or a bad man. (28b)

Philosophy is the love of wisdom; and wisdom is not complex but simple. That does not mean it is easy; simplicity is much harder than complexity. To have a heart that seeks and loves and wills only one thing—the true and the good (which for Socrates are ultimately one)—is difficult and rare. But therein lies wisdom. To have a divided heart that is given to many things—that is easy. Any animal can do that. To worry about a hundred little things is easy, but it does not make us happy or wise or good.

By ordinary standards Socrates is unwise: simple-minded, single-minded, and simplistic, in fact, a fanatic. He has unlimited, infinite passion for just one thing: the good and the true.

By Socrates' standards, it is we who are unwise, for we worry about a relatively unimportant thing, like whether we will live or die, more than the absolutely important thing, whether we do good or evil. He would agree with G. K. Chesterton that "Life is indeed terribly complicated—to a man who has lost his principles."

I think most of us experience in ourselves a double reaction to this single-mindedness of Socrates. On the one hand, we are suspicious, perhaps even cynical. Life cannot be that simple, we think. Socrates lacks "realism" and "sophistication" and "nuance". On the other hand, we recognize him as a *better* man than ourselves; we admire him and perhaps even envy him, for this single passion is the signature of a saint and a martyr. In which of these two reactions is wisdom?

(How wonderfully Socrates works as a touchstone or a mirror! In relation to him we see ourselves more clearly—*whichever* way we answer the question.)

21. *Philosophy is polemical*

"Polemical" means, literally, "warlike". Philosophy is polemical not only because it argues and engages in verbal combat, but above all because it is constantly fighting against ignorance, prejudice, passion, folly, self-deception, and other forces of darkness, both in yourself, when you philosophize, and in your dialogue partners, your society, and the human race.

Socrates describes philosophy as a military obligation given to him by the god. It is **"where God posted** [a military term] **me, as I thought and believed, with the duty to be a philosopher and to test myself and others,** [and not to] **fear either death or anything else, and desert my post"** (28ef). Philosophy is a *jihad*: the Arabic term in the Qur'an means "inner struggle" or "spiritual warfare against evil". Philosophy is not a war against human bodies, and its weapons are not swords or guns. It is a war against the forces that harm human souls (minds and wills), and its weapons are the love of wisdom and the "Socratic method" of logical cross-examination.

Philosophy is not a job; it is a vocation. It is not a private "interest"; it is a response to a call to enlist.

22. *Philosophy is therapeutic*

One of psychotherapy's main uses is to free us from fears. Probably our greatest fear is the fear of death, for in death we seem to lose *everything*. Philosophy as Socrates preaches and practices it frees us from the fear of death.

One way it does this is by teaching us the paradox that **"no evil can happen to a good man either living or dead."** We shall see later what Socrates means by this. It involves a positive insight into what we are, an answer to "know thyself" as the soul rather than the body and, therefore, an understanding of what can and cannot harm us. But there is also another way philosophizing can free us from fear of death, without any positive insight into the nature of self or of death at all, but just by Lesson One:

For to fear death, gentlemen, is only to think you are wise when you are not; for it is to think you know what you don't know. No one knows whether death is really the greatest blessing a man can have, but they fear it is the greatest curse, as if they knew well. Surely this is the objectionable kind of ignorance, to think one knows what one does not know? (29ab)

Socrates draws this therapeutic consequence from Lesson One (that wisdom is to know that you lack wisdom, and folly is to think you have a wisdom that you lack): that hidden in our fear of death is the presupposition that death does us harm and not good; but we do not know that presupposition to be true; so it is foolish, not wise, to fear death.

We naturally react to this with skepticism. But why? Because fear of death is so natural and common. But that does not make it wise! Selfishness and laziness and cowardice are also natural to us and common, but no part of wisdom.

But, we may object, Socrates is presupposing something here, too, something uncommon and apparently unnatural, contrary to human nature. To see what it is, examine the following argument. Socrates says, truly, that we do not know what comes after death. (We do not *know* it. We may believe or hope or fear something—heaven, hell, annihilation, reincarnation—but we do not *know* it.) From this fact he draws the conclusion that we should not fear it. The assumption of the argument is that we should not fear the unknown. But, we reply, this is exactly why we do fear death: it is "the great unknown". It is natural to fear the unknown.

But is it wise? Socrates loves the unknown rather than fearing it. That is almost the definition, the essence of a good learner. Children who at an early age are punished for exploring the unknown will find it hard later to trust their own curiosity and will prefer the safety of the known, like scared rabbits afraid to come out of their comfortable holes. Children who have been encouraged to question and explore the unknown, and rewarded for doing so, will make good students, make many discoveries, and be happy doing so. The unknown is to them not like poison but like food.

This is true. But Socrates' argument forgets that death is not just the *unknown*, it is *death*. We know that life is good, and that death is the loss of this known good, whether something better comes after death or not. Fear of a known loss of a known good does not seem unwise.

23. Philosophy is "conformist"

Of course Socrates is a rebel, a nonconformist. That is why he is executed. So why do I say philosophy is "conformist"?

Because the only reason why Socrates noncon-forms to his accusers is because he conforms to the god. He disobeys the will of the Athenians only because he must obey the will of God. It is not his own private autonomy or will-to-power that he asserts.

He is this offensive thing, a philosopher, out of obedient piety:

If you were to say to me in answer to this: "We will not this time listen to Anytos, my dear Socrates; we will let you go free, but on this condition, that you will no longer spend your time in this search or in philosophy, and if you are caught doing this again, you shall die"—if you should let me go free on these terms which I have mentioned, I should answer you, "Many thanks indeed for your kindness, gentlemen, but I will obey the god rather than you, and as long as I have breath in me, and remain able to do it, I will never cease being a philosopher. (29cd)

Note the almost exact equivalent in Acts 5:29, where the same disobedience to legal, social authority is justified, in the face of death, by the same words: "We must obey God rather than men."

It is often thought that religious believers are "conservative" while atheists and skeptics are "radicals" or "progressives", but it is the other way around: those who believe in a higher standard can justify social disobedience and rebellion, but those who do not must see society as the source of law and the definer of the good, and thus divinize society; and this is status-quo conservatism and conformism.

An individual has three possible standards for living, and when any two of them conflict, one must be conformed to (obeyed) and the other not conformed to (disobeyed). The three are (1) that which is higher than man, (2) that which is man-made, and (3) that which is less than man. The first standard is something higher in value, and in authority, than human society or individuals, some God or gods, or at least something with divine attributes and therefore divine authority: eternal, perfect, and absolute. The second standard is society, that is, human beings in a community, whether democratic or not. This standard is created by human wills, whether by consensus or majority vote or the will of the one or the few. The third possible standard is any natural forces less than the human will, for example, fear, animal instincts, passions, and so on—something subrational.

Philosophy as Socrates understands it is by its nature drawn to the first of these three because philosophy is the love of wisdom, and wisdom, like truth, goodness, and even beauty, is an ideal that judges us, rather than an artifact or human product that we judge. We want to live according to wisdom and to change our lives to conform to it, not change it to conform to our lives.

And this makes it possible for the philosopher to be a nonconformist to, a judge of, and a rebel against the other two standards: the will of society and his own subrational nature and instincts. Socrates is just such a philosopher.

24. *Philosophy is embarrassing*

Because it seeks wisdom and judges us by this higher standard, philosophy embarrasses us, as a strong light embarrasses us by revealing the warts and pimples behind our makeup. It says to us, as Socrates said to his fellow Athenians, and keeps saying to them and to us even after he is dead:

My excellent friend, you are an Athenian [or an American], **a citizen of this great city, so famous for wisdom and strength, and you take every care to be as well off as possible in money, reputation and place—then are you not ashamed not to take every care and thought for understanding, for truth, and for the soul, that it may be perfect? And if any of you argues the point and says he does take every care, I will not at once let him go and depart myself; but I will question and cross-examine and test him, and if I think he does not possess virtue but only says so, I will show that he sets very little value on things most precious, and sets more value on meaner things, and I will put him to shame. This I will do for everyone I meet, young or old, native or foreigner ... for this is what God commands me.** (29d–30a)

When a light puts you to shame, you want to put it out. This is why Athens killed Socrates and why we habitually do the same to great sages, from Jesus to Gandhi.

But can we kill the Socrates within us?

25. Philosophy is invulnerable

And it makes the *philosopher* invulnerable! Of all the strange and striking things Socrates says in his *Apology*, the strangest and the most striking of all is this point. He knows it will seem very strange, so he prefaces it with a sentence in which he repeats four times his plea to hear this point and not to drown it with

scorn: **"Don't make an uproar, gentlemen, remain
quiet as I begged you, hear me without uproar
at what I have to say; for I think it will be to your
benefit to hear me. I have something more to say,
which perhaps will make you shout, but I pray
you, don't do so."** (30c)

What point will be so offensive and outrageous?
It will be (a) one of Socrates' paradoxes, something
apparently very obviously false, (b) one that "will be
to our benefit to hear", a very practical, important,
in fact life-changing point, and (c) one of the few
things Socrates ever claims to be certain of. In fact,
his next words are, **"Be sure of this"**—words he
hardly ever speaks, especially right after he has revealed that his claim to wisdom is that he does *not*
know what others think they know. (However, the
other aspect of his wisdom is that he *does* know what
others do not.)

The point is so important that he repeats it in the
very last paragraph of his speech, as his dying gift to
the world, and there, too (41c), he claims it is something we **"must take as true"**, that is, certain. Yet it
is an outrageous paradox. What is it?

The last paragraph of the *Apology* expresses it as a
general principle: **"No evil can happen to a good
man either living or dead."** The earlier passage
expresses its application to one particular individual—himself—in this particular situation—facing a
death sentence: **"Be sure of this, that if you put
me to death, being such as I am, you will not hurt
me so much as yourselves. I should** [British for
would] **not be hurt either by Meletos or by Anytos, he could not do it; for I think the eternal law**

[*logos*] **forbids a better man to be hurt by a worse"** (30cd).

Classical Greek has two words for "law". One of them, *nomos*, means a law enacted by man, like "Do not commit treason, and if you do, we will kill you if we catch you." *Nomoi* can be disobeyed, and are, for they express the will of some men over others, and human wills can choose to disobey. The other word for "law", *logos*, means an eternal law, a law of the nature of things, which simply *cannot* be broken— for example, $2 + 3 = 5$, or $E = mc^2$.

And Socrates calls this principle that **"forbids a better man to be hurt by a worse"** a *logos*.

But he, Socrates, the innocent victim of Anytos, Meletos, and Lycon, is a better man. And they, the victimizers, are worse men. Socrates stands right in the middle of the classic case of the better man being harmed by the worse and says it can never happen! To the world's most agonizing question, which has tortured the minds of the wise, namely, the "problem of evil", "why bad things happen to good people", Socrates answers, "they never do." The answer seems so cavalier, so naïve, so outrageous that we understand why Socrates has to plead for silence. (**"Don't make an uproar."**) But do we understand why he believes it?

Socrates himself gives us a clue in his next words: **"However, he might put me to death, or banish me, or make me outcast; perhaps he thinks, perhaps others think, these are great evils, but I do not; I think, rather, that what he is now doing is evil, when he tries unjustly to put a man to death"** (30d).

Evidently, Socrates means something very different by "evil" from what his accusers do. He means something we *do*; they mean something we *suffer*. He means sin; they mean pain. He means spiritual evil; they mean physical evil.

But this is not just a difference about the use of words. It is a different philosophy of one's very identity. The explanation of Socrates' paradox is very simple, many would say even simplistic: Socrates had solved the oracle's oldest riddle, "Know thyself" (*gnothi seauton*). He had discovered what he was. *That* is the connection, the middle term, between "know thyself" and **"no evil can happen to a good man"**. A man's self is not his body but his soul.

The Greek word we translate "soul" (*psychē*) meant "ghost" to most of Socrates' contemporaries. That is what it meant in Homer and Hesiod. When a warrior dies, he is buried, but his ghost lives on in the underworld, a shadowy "realm of the dead", not of the living. A man's ghost (*psychē*) is to a man almost what a "ghost image" on a TV screen, which appears for a moment after you turn it off, is to the live TV show. Socrates' contemporaries thought he was implying that a man's real self was his ghost.

But Socrates was using the old word in a radical new sense (as the writers of the New Testament would do four centuries later with the Greek word *agapē*, "love"). For Socrates, your nonphysical self, your thinking and choosing self, is more real, more solid and substantial, and certainly more long-lasting, than your body. In fact, it is immortal. Socrates is really the first person who used "soul" in the modern sense.

Or, more accurately, we have not yet caught up

with Socrates. We are still pre-Socratics, at least in our spontaneous imagery. For we imagine the soul as something like a gas, or a ghost, or an ectoplasm, thin and wispy like a fog. (This is the image movies, TV, and comics always use: when a character dies, his "ghost" rises from his body.) If Socrates were to use a concrete image for the soul, it would not be something thin and ephemeral like a fog or a rainbow but something solid and heavy like a bar of iron. The soul is invulnerable to evil from without, from the physical world. You cannot kill a soul. The only evil that can harm a soul is spiritual evil, moral evil; but this is something only the individual can do to himself. No one and nothing outside me can make me foolish and vicious; I alone can do that. You can harm my body, but only I can harm my soul (cf. Mt 15:10–20).

And the wise man knows himself, knows that he is his soul. And thus he is invulnerable. His pursuit of wisdom, his philosophy, has made him invulnerable (or, rather, has discovered his invulnerability).

There are two very different possible criticisms of this idea of Socrates that a man *is* his soul. On the one hand, we may, quite fairly and realistically, criticize him for ignoring the profound "psychosomatic unity" of soul and body, the spiritual meaning of the body (is the body our machine?), and the fact that we can harm others' souls through their bodies, by tempting them to evil or by making it much harder for them to choose the good by inflicting physical pain on them. Socrates has just discovered a profound and precious truth; we should not expect him to discover also its almost-opposite truth, or at least its qualifications and nuancings.

But, on the other hand, we may simply *not see* what Socrates sees. We may reduce soul to ghost, mind to brain, thinking to computing, love to lust, morality to mores, beauty to titillation; and then when we say that bad men can indeed harm good men, we think we have simply refuted Socrates and shown his "wisdom" to be folly. If we are that kind of materialist, we are the fools, who have not yet learned who we are in the most primary way. (The *first* kind of criticism of Socrates, by contrast, accepts this primary discovery of his but adds important secondary ones to his concept of "self".)

Despite all the reservations and qualifications we may want to add to it, Socrates' basic point retains the power to convince and inspire, to change minds and even lives "radically", that is, at their root.

26. Philosophy is annoying

Socrates uses the very unflattering image of a biting insect (a gadfly, or horsefly) to describe the philosopher. No wonder the horse responds by swatting this insect away:

For if you put me to death, you will not easily find such another, really like something stuck on the state by the god, though it is rather laughable to say so; for the state is like a big thoroughbred horse, so big that he is a bit slow and heavy, and wants a gadfly to wake him up. I think the god put me on the state something like that, to wake you up and persuade you and reproach you every one, as I keep settling on you everywhere all day

long. . . . You will be vexed, perhaps, like sleepers being awakened, and if you listen to Anytos and gave me a tap, you can easily kill me; then you can go on sleeping for the rest of your lives. (30e–31a)

When the alarm clock buzzes in the morning, do you have warm, sweet, comfortable feelings of gratitude toward it? When you are sleeping in the hammock and a bug bite wakes you up, do you smile at the bug and say, "Thanks, I needed that"?

If you do not annoy anyone, you are not a philosopher.

27. *Philosophy is pneumatic*

Pneuma is the Greek word for "spirit"—and also for "breath" or "air". (A single word also performs this same double duty in Hebrew: *ruah*.) Not all philosophers can expect to experience the remarkable "inspiration" (literally, "in-breathing") of the Spirit that Socrates speaks of in the *Apology*, but all can expect some. (This is a point that I have never seen made in any book that tries to introduce philosophy.)

Who or what is this "Spirit"? That is a mystery to the reader of the *Apology*, for it seems to have been a mystery to Socrates, too. But it was real, not imaginary; that seems clear. For the mark of anything real is action: real things act and cause effects; they change other things, while figments of our imagination, mind, or speech do not: they are effects (of imagining or thinking or speaking) but not causes. We cause them. And this "**something divine and spiritual**" that Socrates speaks of acts on Socrates.

That is clear, though remarkable. Even more remarkable, we find a somewhat similar phenomenon in our own thought-life when we philosophize.

Let us first look at Socrates' experience and then at ours.

He says he did not

> dare . . . appear before your public assembly and advise the state. The reason for this is one which you have often heard me giving in many places, that something divine and spiritual comes to me, which Meletos put into the indictment in caricature. This has been about me since my boyhood, a voice, which when it comes always turns me away from doing something I am intending to do, but never urges me on. This is what opposes my taking up public business. And quite right too, I think; for you may be sure, gentlemen, that if I had meddled with public business in the past, I should have perished long ago and done no good either to you or to myself. (31c–e)

Later in the trial, after Socrates has given his uncompromising and unrepentant speech and received the uncompromising verdict of death, he mentions this "**something divine and spiritual**" again:

> My familiar prophetic voice of the spirit in all time past has always come to me frequently, opposing me even in very small things, if I was about to do something not right; but now there has happened to me what you see yourselves, what one might

think and what is commonly held to be the extremest of evils, yet for me, as I left home this morning, there was no opposition from the signal of God, nor when I entered this place of the court, nor anywhere in my speech when I was about to say anything; although in other speeches of mine it has often checked me while I was still speaking, yet now in this action it has not opposed me anywhere, either in deed or in word. Then what am I to conceive to be the cause? I will tell you: really this that has happened to me is good, and it is impossible that any of us conceives it aright who thinks it is an evil thing to die. A strong proof of this has been given to me; for my usual signal would certainly have opposed me, unless I was about to do something good. (40a–c)

It is tempting to identify this "spirit" or "prophetic voice", or "signal of God" that Socrates claims to have with something familiar. To reduce the unfamiliar to the familiar relieves the strangeness, the wonder; but **philosophy begins in wonder** (*Theaetetus* 155d).

One familiar category we might be tempted to use to explain Socrates "hearing voices" is schizophrenia—but only if we are unfamiliar with schizophrenia, with Socrates, and with the enormous contrast between these two things in a thousand other ways.

Could it have been his *conscience*? Perhaps Socrates simply had a very sensitive conscience. Many believe that conscience is in fact the voice of God, God's inner prophet in each soul. (That would explain why even moral relativists, moral subjectivists, and moral skeptics do not approve any individual deliberately disobeying his own conscience, ever. Conscience is treated as having absolute, divine authority even by relativists and atheists.) And conscience seems to "speak" almost with a "voice".

No, it will not do. Socrates' "spirit" could not be conscience. (1) For all men have a conscience, but this "spirit" sets Socrates apart. (2) And conscience gives us positive as well as negative guidance, but this "spirit" only forbids, never commands. (3) And a good man's well-exercised conscience speaks many times every day, while this "spirit" seems to speak only on some special occasions. (4) Furthermore, conscience is moral *reason*, moral insights, moral understanding; but this "spirit" gives no reasons. (5) Also, conscience, being a human power, is fallible and ought to be questioned and trained, especially if you are Socrates, who questions everything; but Socrates obeys this "spirit" blindly and absolutely without doubts or questions—*most* uncharacteristic behavior for him! (6) Above all, conscience is "inside" us; it speaks *from* us. But this "spirit" comes *to* Socrates from without.

I can think of only two candidates that fit this description. If you are a pagan, you could believe it is a god, most likely Apollo, the god of the oracle. If you are a Jew, a Muslim, or a Christian, you could believe it is the Spirit of God, what Christians call the Holy Spirit. (It could have also been an angel, God's intermediary.) Why could he not have spoken to Socrates? Why are we so ready to limit what God can do?

But what does this theological speculation about Socrates have to do with philosophy and with us?

Just a suggestion, hopefully one provocative of thought: Do you know where your best thoughts come from?

You have already philosophized, whoever you are, for the pursuit of wisdom is innate to human nature. You have often said, "the thought came into my mind . . ." It is much easier to know where your ordinary thoughts come from—your conscious mind and will—than where your wisest "inspirations" come from. The deeper the thought, the darker its source. How much do you know, really, about the invisible, spiritual "pneumatic" sources of this great Nile river we call thought, which waters the whole Egypt of your life? If you are not an atheist, you must think it at least possible, perhaps even likely, that Socrates' unusually explicit connection with **"something divine and spiritual"**, and your connection with it, too, are both real rather than being the egotistic self-deception that it must be if is *not* God but only yourself.

It is probably impossible to prove one way or the other. So what difference would it make to the philosopher? He could be more sensitive and open, silent and listening, to this source and develop a habit of receptivity. And, qua human being now rather than qua philosopher, he might want to turn to and thank Socrates' "unknown god" for these precious but anonymous gifts. No wise man in history has ever put a small value on gratitude. Even Martin Heidegger, who was an agnostic (some claim an atheist), pointed to the near identity in German between *denken* (thinking) and *danken* (thanking).

28. *Philosophy is apolitical*

By this I do not mean that philosophers are politically irrelevant or do not make political judgments,
general or particular, or create political philosophies,
but that philosophy does not stem from politics; philosophy's sources are deeper than politics; philosophy
is not the instrument of politics.

Because philosophy will not serve politics, and because politics is often a jealous and tyrannical master, philosophers often clash with political forces,
sometimes even fatally, as did Socrates. He knows
this:

> **The fact is that no man in the world will
> come off safe who honestly opposes either
> you or any other multitude** [democracy, too,
> can be totalitarian], **and tries to hinder the
> many unjust and illegal doings in a state. It
> is necessary that one who really and truly
> fights for the right, if he is to survive even for
> a short time, shall act as a private man, not
> as a public man.** (31e–32a)

29. *Philosophy is docile (teachable)*

Socrates, the world's greatest teacher, says,

> **I never was teacher to anyone; but if anyone
> desires to hear me speaking and doing my
> business, whether he be young or old, I have
> never grudged it to any ... I offer myself
> both to rich and poor for questioning, and if
> a man likes he may hear what I say, and an-**

swer. And whether anyone becomes good after this or not, I could not fairly be called the cause of it. (33ab)

Because the philosopher is a lover of wisdom, he is always a pupil, a student. In Socrates' concept of philosophy, the roles of teacher and student are reversed: the teacher becomes the student and questions the student, who must then teach. For the assumption in asking a question is that the person who is asked has knowledge of the answer.

Any experienced teacher will tell you he has learned more from the teacher's side of the desk than he ever did from the student's side.

A teacher cannot put ideas into the student's mind as a parent can put food into a baby's mouth. To learn requires great activity: the activity of receptivity to, and love of, truth. The ancients called this "docility", which means literally, "teachability". It is not passivity; it is the opposite of passivity. Passive minds are *not* teachable; only active minds are.

30. Philosophy is messianic

"A messiah complex" sounds as far as possible from the humility and docility we have seen associated with Socrates' concept of philosophy. What is meant here?

That philosophy, as exemplified by Socrates, fulfills the confused but prophetic promises or anticipations of it in earlier Greek myth and religion. For look what Socrates says about the source of this new thing he is doing that will bring about his own martyrdom for the crime of atheism: **"I maintain that I**

**have been commanded by the god to do this,
through oracles and dreams and in every way in
which some divine influence or other has ever
commanded a man to do anything**" (33c). (Read
that again, slowly!)

Socrates is here claiming to be something like the
messiah of his people. The claim is probably meant
not for himself but for philosophy; but the claim is
astonishingly bold: that all authentic revelations of
the gods culminate here; all the public mythologies
and private oracles are here fulfilled. Socrates has all
heaven's phone lines running through his house.

In the mouth of any other man, this would automatically be labeled overweening pride and absurd
egotism. But it is the combination of personal humility with the enormity of the claim that makes it
unique. The only comparable juxtaposition, of an
even greater claim and an even greater personal self-
effacement (also to the point of voluntary martyrdom) is with Jesus, who of course also claimed to be
his people's Messiah, the one promised and pointed
to by all the prophets.

And both claims, Socrates' claim in philosophy and
Jesus' claim in religion, though they come from particular individuals in particular cultures, are claims
to universal truth for all humanity and all cultures.

And no two individuals' claims have, in historical
fact, been accepted and acted upon by more of humanity than the claims of these two. Subtract either
Socrates or Jesus from history, and you leave more
absences, greater changes, than can be imagined by
the best science fiction writers in the world.

31. *Philosophy is pious*

Just before the jury votes on his guilt as a nonbeliever in the gods of the state, Socrates claims, "**I do believe, in a sense in which none of my accusers does**" (35d). What does he mean by this, and what does it have to do with the very nature of philosophy?

Socrates is not shuffling. The "**sense in which none of my accusers does**" believe, but Socrates does, is *not* a weaker but a stronger sense in two ways.

First, the god Socrates believes in—always "*the* god" (*ho theos*), in the singular, when he is serious, not the plural, and always unnamed, never identified with any of the gods of the state—this god is greater, stronger, more able to receive belief, and a more total belief. This is so whether this "god" exists or not. The point is psychological, not theological. Socrates' god is a god one can "believe in" in a far deeper, more total sense than any of the gods of the state. For no one in Athens was ever a martyr for Athena or Apollo or Zeus.

Socrates' belief in "the god" behind the oracle was so great that he changed his life because of it. He became a philosopher because he *believed* the message from the oracle, that no one in the world was wiser than he, though he could not *understand* it. He gave his life to the enterprise of trying to understand it, by developing the art of "Socratic method" philosophizing, and then gave up his life because this enterprise of philosophizing (which he always calls "the god's task", "the god's command", and so on) offended the believers in the gods of the state. Indeed, he does believe in a sense in which none of his accusers does.

Secondly, Socrates' belief is greater because it is philosophical and it wants to know; it treats truth as the supreme god and loves this god absolutely, at any cost. Even an atheist can be pious or religious in this sense, if he "believes in" and loves and pursues and steers his life absolutely by truth; if he is an atheist because he believes atheism is *true*.

Socrates *was* an atheist, or at least an agnostic, regarding the gods of the state; yet he believed in a deeper sense than the religious believers who condemned him. They believed in their gods because this was socially acceptable, culturally "appropriate", and profitable. They did not question their beliefs, but questioned Socrates' questioning of their beliefs. They were more concerned with Socrates than with truth; Socrates was more concerned with truth than with them, or their gods, or his life.

This is the Socratic essence of philosophy: devotion to truth above all, truth as God. Thus philosophy is pious, even for an atheist.

If Socrates is right about God, the less than totally honest theist will require a longer Purgatory than the totally honest atheist, for he has not yet graduated from God's kindergarten.

32. *Philosophy is impractical*

Socrates describes the life of the philosopher (himself) this way:

> **. . . neglecting what most people care about, moneymaking and housekeeping and military appointments and oratory, and besides, all the posts and plots and parties which arise**

**in this city. . . . I tried to persuade each one
of you to take care for himself first, and how
he could become most good and most wise,
before he took care of any of her inter-
ests. . . . (36bc)**

"Philosophy bakes no bread", says the cynical
cliché. To which Socrates would reply, as another
wise man once did to the temptation to prefer "practical" things like bread to wisdom, "Man does not live
by bread alone." That man also uttered the most
practical sentence ever spoken: "What does it profit
a man if he gain the whole world and lose his own
soul?"

That is Socrates' point, too: Our most practical
need is to be more than a pragmatist.

A standard joke-shop item is the little black box:
when you move the lever from "off" to "on", it
whirrs, blinks a red light, and opens a trap door in
its top, allowing a hand to come out and shut its lever
off, then drop back into the box. Every part of the
box is practical—it has a purpose beyond itself—the
battery sends energy along the wire; the wire takes it
to a gear; the gear turns; it opens the top; and so on—
but there is absolutely no reason or purpose to the
box as a whole. That is why it is so funny.

But a life like that, a life composed only of practical things that serve some other end but with nothing in it worth having for its own sake—the true,
the good, the beautiful—such a life is not funny but
pitiful.

It is philosophy, the pursuit of wisdom, that demands a higher life than that. The purpose of life, the
end to which all practical things are means, cannot

be itself a practical thing, a means to a further end. What that purpose is, is a question for philosophy. It is an "impractical" question, but the most important one of all.

33. Philosophy is happy

"**Any one of you who has gained the prize at Olympia ... makes you seem to be happy, but I make you be happy**" (36d). For philosophy questions appearances to find truth, including true happiness.

The very achievement itself of finding truth for its own sake makes us happy, for that is what we are made for, that is what satisfies our distinctively human desire. Truth is to the soul what food is to the body.

Socrates does not seem to make people happy. He makes them angry—so angry that they kill him. But sometimes true happiness can only come through apparent unhappiness. If we do not philosophize, if we do not question appearances, if we are satisfied with whatever makes us *feel* happy, we will never know whether we are being deceived about who we are and what level of our being is being satisfied.

34. Philosophy is necessary

Philosophy is not like fishing or painting or jogging: it is not simply a good thing for some people to do. It is necessary, and it is universal. To be human is to be challenged to philosophize, and if we respond by not philosophizing, then that is our philosophy, a bad one. Once Romeo proposes to Juliet, she is no longer innocent, but involved, whether she answers Yes or

No. Once we are rational, philosophy proposes to us, and we are no longer innocent, like the animals.

In just two sentences Socrates gives three reasons why it is necessary to philosophize: It is commanded by "the god"; and it is "the greatest good", the *summum bonum*; and therefore a life without it is "not worth living for a man" (as distinct from an ostrich):

Perhaps someone might say, Can't you go away from us, Socrates, and keep silent and lead a quiet life? Now here is the most difficult thing of all to make some of you believe. For if I say that this is to disobey the god, and therefore I cannot keep quiet, you will not believe me but think I am a humbug. If again I say it is the greatest good for a man every day to discuss virtue and the other things, about which you hear me talking and examining myself and everybody else, and that life without enquiry is not worth living for a man, you will believe me still less if I say that. And yet all this is true, gentlemen, as I tell you, but to convince you is not easy. (37e–38a)

Although Socrates' first reason (the god's command) may seem to apply to him alone, it is as universal as the other two. For (1) the god Socrates obeyed was evidently not one of the local gods of Athens only, but *"the* god", the one God of all men, including the reader of these words. And (2) this God's intention was clearly to put Socrates onto the state like a gadfly (30e) and thus onto the whole world; to spread the good infection of philosophy from his chosen apostle Socrates whom he first in-

fected. This is why Socrates cannot simply philosophize quietly and privately, but must make a pest of
himself: he is a missionary (though his religion con-
sists chiefly of questions, of "inquiry").

35. *Philosophy is death-defying*

"It's a matter of life or death!" These are the words
that rouse us the most. But philosophy questions
even this. It does not accept the position that is as-
signed to almost everything else in human life,
namely, to be under death's sway, under death's judg-
ment. Instead it judges death from a higher standard.
From the viewpoint of wisdom, "it's a matter of good
or evil" trumps "it's a matter of life or death."

Socrates could have escaped with his life if he had
only admitted guilt (which would have been to lie)
and wept and pleaded with his accusers. But bodily
death is not the greatest evil, and bodily life is not
the greatest good. Therefore he says:

> **Neither in court nor in war ought I or any-
> one else to do anything and everything to
> contrive an escape from death. In battle it
> is often clear that a man might escape by
> throwing away his arms and by begging
> mercy from his pursuers; and there are many
> other means in every danger, for escaping
> death, if a man can bring himself to do and
> say anything and everything. No, gentlemen,
> the difficult thing is not to escape death, I
> think, but to escape wickedness—that is
> much more difficult, for that runs faster than
> death. And now I, being slow and old, have
> been caught by the slower one; but my ac-**

cusers, being clever and quick, have been caught by the swifter, badness. And now I and they depart, I, condemned by you to death, but these, condemned by truth to depravity and injustice. I abide by my penalty, they by theirs. (38e–39b)

Notice the contrast: Socrates' judges are unjust mortals; their judge is immortal truth. From the viewpoint of these men, they have tried, condemned, and destroyed philosophy. But from the viewpoint of philosophy, as incarnated by Socrates, they have only done this to themselves, that is, to their true selves, their souls. They seem to be judging Socrates, but behind the appearances the real truth is that he is judging them, simply by being what he is.

The same ironic reversal can be seen in the trial of Jesus. His judge, Pilate, showed the same philosophical face as Socrates' judges by his scornful question, "What is truth?" Pilate thought he was judging truth, but truth was judging him.

When a man refuses to philosophize honestly, that is, to seek wisdom (truth about good and evil), and turns his face away from the light of truth, he walks into his own shadow. Truth is never on trial; we are.

Philosophy is death-defying because it is friendship with truth, and truth is stronger than death. This becomes clear to us when we come close to death:

I wish to chant this prophecy to you whose votes have condemned me; for I am now in the place where men chiefly prophesy, in sight of coming death. I foretell, gentlemen, my slayers, that a punishment will come upon you straight after my death, much

harder, I declare, than execution at your hands is to me; for now you have done this, thinking to shake yourselves free from giving account of your life, but it will turn out for you something very different, as I foretell. More than one shall be those who demand from you that account. (39c)

When a man approaches death, he approaches eternity; that is why he often receives a gift of prophecy then; for only from the viewpoint of eternity can the future be known. Socrates' prophecy came true, both in Athens immediately after Socrates' death and throughout the world for the rest of time, wherever the name of Socrates lived on.

As Socrates will point out in the *Phaedo*, philosophy is a rehearsal, or "practice" (*meletē*), for death, for philosophy seeks eternal truth. Philosophy is a river, restless until it reaches the timeless sea. Why should the philosopher fear death? The philosopher seeks truth, and death is *more truth*.

36. Philosophy is fallible

Philosophy is human, not divine. Therefore, it is fallible. It *seeks* wisdom, implying that it does not yet possess it. Truth is divine; the love of it is human.

Therefore we can expect even Socrates to make mistakes. And he seems to make a pretty big one in his argument for the conclusion (at 40d–41a), that we should not fear death. The conclusion may be true, but his argument for it is weak. The conclusion he is arguing for is that **"it is impossible that any of us conceives it aright who think it is an evil thing to die"** (40bc). And his argument is this:

Death is one of two things; either the dead man is nothing, and has no consciousness of anything at all, or it is, as people say, a change and a migration for the soul from this place here to another place. If there is no consciousness and it is like a sleep, when [the] one sleeping sees nothing, not even in dreams, death would be a wonderful blessing. . . . But if, again, death is a migration from this world into another place, and if what they say is true, that there all the dead are, what greater good could there be than this . . . ? For if one comes to the house of Hades [the world of the dead], **rid of those who dub themselves judges, and finds those who truly are judges, . . . would that migration be a poor thing?** (40c–41a)

There are two things wrong with this argument. First, no one prefers sleep and unconsciousness to waking consciousness unless he is in misery. If Socrates' second possibility (death is "**migration**" to another place, with continued consciousness) is good, then his other possibility (*deprivation* of this good by eternal *lack* of consciousness) is *not* good, not "**a wonderful blessing**".

Second, Socrates' second possibility (death as "migration") *assumes* that life after death will be both just (since there are good judges there) and happy (since the other dead are there). But he gives no proof for this hope. There are other possibilities that he does not consider: that life after death is unhappy because the judges there are *not* just or good or in charge; or that it is unhappy for *us* because they are just, and we get the punishments we deserved but escaped in this life; or that we are incapable of enjoying the goodness of the gods as a flea is incapable of enjoying the sun or the sea.

In other words, what awaits us after death is either annihilation, heaven, hell, or Purgatory. Socrates idealizes annihilation and ignores hell and Purgatory, even though his own culture's myths contained versions of them.

Socrates would be surprised at us if we were surprised at his fallibility. If there is any one lesson he would have us learn, it is to question and examine every idea, including his. He would agree with St. Paul's two-step maxim "test everything; hold fast what is good" (1 Thess 5:21). How can we know we are doing the second unless we are doing the first?

37. *Philosophy is immortal*

Philosophy is not just for this life. If there is an afterlife and if we are human there, we are philosophers there too. Thus Socrates' hope for heaven is **"to go on cross-examining the people there, as I did those here"** (41b). One advantage of being a philosopher rather than a soldier or an economist or a lawyer or a doctor is that you have job security even after death. It makes little sense to hope for a heaven that contains soldiers (that is, wars), economists (that is, poverty), lawyers (that is, injustices), or doctors (that is, disease). But philosophers, artists, musicians— they are even now doing heavenly things.

Even death will not change Socrates. He is a bit like a god that way. For the Greeks, the first mark of a god was immortality. Even though Socrates would be gazing at eternal truth in heaven, he could at the same time be exercising the acts of charity that he exercised on earth, namely, helping others to come closer to this truth by cross-examining them.

You may think it would not be heavenly to have to endure the cross-examinations of a Socrates; but this objection would reveal more about you than about heaven. It would reveal how you experience Socrates and philosophy as pain rather than pleasure, as his accusers did rather than his friends. If so, Socrates' heaven and your Purgatory may turn out to be the same place—until you learn to love this heavenly thing and become able to enjoy it.

Why not begin now?

38. Philosophy is confident

There are two kinds of confidence, or trust. One kind is a *hope*; the other is a *certainty*.

Socrates has the first kind of confidence toward death. He has risked his life on death being good, not evil, and on there being good judges in the afterlife and the opportunity for him to go on cross-examining people there. Yet he calls this only a hope, not a certainty. But in the same sentence he tells us what we *can* be certain of: **"In that world they are happier than we are here . . . , if what people say is true. But you also, judges of the court, must have good hopes towards death, and this one thing you must take as true—no evil can happen to a good man either living or dead"** (41cd).

Before exiting to die, Socrates leaves us with this one great gift, which can make us as confident as he even in the face of death. It is not the weak argument above (point 36) that gives us this confidence. No, it is more than a "hope"; it is a necessary truth ("**this one thing you *must* take as true**"). What is it, then?

As we pointed out above (point 25), if you "know yourself", you can know not just *that* it is true, but *why* it is true, why it is necessarily true that "**no evil can happen to a good man**". The connecting link between "know thyself" and "**no evil can happen to a good man**", is the soul. Your self is your soul; and soul evils, or spiritual evils, unlike bodily evils or physical evils, never just "happen" to us. They come from us, not to us. They come by choice, not by chance.

The root of "happen" is "hap", the Middle English word for "chance" or "luck". That is also the root of the modern English word "happiness". This is an indication of how little we know ourselves, how materialistic and externalistic and shallow we habitually are. We think happiness "happens".

If we follow the tutelage of "the love of wisdom" we will eventually reach the Socratic level of self-knowledge in which we understand that true happiness never happens; we are responsible for it, for its cause is (of all things!) virtue.

39. *Philosophy is painful*

Socrates makes one last request, for his children: "**One thing I ask . . . : Punish my sons, gentlemen, when they grow up; give them this same pain I gave you, if you think they care for money or anything else before virtue**" (41e).

Philosophy is good pain. Until we are in heaven,

we need this pain, this Purgatory. For whenever the light of true philosophy meets the darkness of ignorance and vice in us, there must be conflict and pain. When the greatest light and the greatest darkness met, there was a Cross.

And that is the very best place in this world for us to be: in the very best company.

40. *Philosophy is agnostic*

Astonishing as it may sound, it is very frequently necessary to remind ourselves that we are not God.

And therefore we need to end many of our inquiries where Socrates ends the *Apology*: at exactly the same place where he began, "I do not know". His very last words are: "**And now it is time to go, I to die, and you to live; but which of us goes to a better thing is unknown to all but God.**"

Last words are significant, as first words are. Socrates lets God have the last word.

This is not only pious but also philosophical. If we are not Sophists ("wise men") but philosophers ("lovers of wisdom"); if wisdom's home is not here but its loving, longing pursuit is; then in "letting God have the last word" (that is, deliberately ending with the word "God"), Socrates shows that he does "know himself". He is the one who knows that he does not know; God is the one who knows; and the fool is the "Sophist" who does not know that he does not know.

That is philosophy's Lesson One. No philosophy that will not use that runway will ever fly.

Note on the Absence of a Note on the Historical and Cultural Background

How do we know how much of the *Apology* is historical? How much did Socrates actually say, and how much is Plato's invention?

I answer with Socrates' last words of the *Apology*: "Only God knows."

I have deliberately omitted the usual historical and cultural notes and introduction and "explanations" for the *Apology* because these are almost sure to be misused more than used, to reduce rather than to enlarge our data. They will be used to explain away rather than to explain; to "see through" rather than to see; to stand apart from Socrates and philosophy and the Greeks, like a museum curator pointing out his caged, labeled, and very dead exhibits, rather than to enter into Socrates and into philosophy. What we want is not to stand over Socrates but to stand under him, to under-stand him.

Fashionably ironic cultural relativism is the point of view from which most histories of philosophy are written today. The idea of actually meeting Socrates (his ghost, at least), of seeing him as equally contemporary to us and equally relevant and valid today as he was in Athens in 399 B.C.—the idea that this politically incorrect, dead, white, European, heterosexual, religious male could possibly come to us across the centuries and challenge us to see truths and practice virtues that are timeless and universal and not at all outdated or limited to some cultures or some personalities—this idea is far more arresting, more enlightening, and more stimulating to actual engagement in philosophy on the part of the student and reader than the best and most complete possible survey of Socrates' culture and its history.

I have omitted even small technical, historical items such as Athenian trial law and how their wars with Persia and then Sparta weighed on the Athenians, fully realizing that this will render a few aspects of the *Apology* obscure to the beginner. For this sense of obscurity, strangeness, and mystery, the sense that there is more in the thing than in the thought, "more things in heaven and earth than are dreamed of in your philosophy", is precious and increasingly rare. It is precious because with it the student senses that he is a fly exploring an elephant, while without it he thinks he is a computer processing "information". It is rare because outside "Great Books" programs, the humanities today have pretty much fallen into the hands of the Sophists of our time: cultural relativists, "politically correct" deconstructionists, reductionists, determinists, skeptics, and ironic nihilists. And please do not ask me to define all these intellectual obscenities here. There is something doubly obscene about *defining* obscenities. So let us just leave it with this outrageously irresponsible name-calling.

We will, however, "explain" and "contextualize" the *Apology* in another way: using Socrates himself. Plato wrote a dialogue about a conversation Socrates had only a few hours earlier than the *Apology*, on his way to court, with a young man named Euthyphro, on the topic of religious piety; and another dialogue about a conversation Socrates had a few days later, in prison just before he died, with some of his disciples, on the topic of life after death, on the immortality of the soul. The parts of these two dialogues (*Euthyphro* and *Phaedo*) that most reveal Socrates and his concept and practice of philosophy are given here as a context for the *Apology*. The *Euthyphro* shows why Socrates was hated and killed; the *Phaedo* shows how he died. The *Apology* only *tells* about these two things; these other two dialogues *show* them.

II

From the *Euthyphro*: Philosophy Exemplified

This dialogue (or rather the beginning of it) is included here to show the reader three things:

1. Socrates in action: how and why he offended people without being an offensive person

2. The "Socratic" method in action, the nature of logical cross-examination, especially the search for a definition of a thing's essence

3. An introduction to the issue of the relation between philosophy and religion, reason and faith—an issue central to every historical era including our own

EUTHYPHRO: This, Socrates, is something new? What has taken you from your haunts in the Lyceum, and makes you spend your time at the royal porch? You surely cannot have a case at law, as I have, before the Archon-King. 2

SOCRATES: My business, Euthyphro, is not what is known at Athens as a case at law; it is a criminal prosecution.

EUTHYPHRO: How is that? You mean that some- b

body is prosecuting you? I never would believe that you were prosecuting anybody else.

SOCRATES: No indeed.

EUTHYPHRO: Then somebody is prosecuting you?

SOCRATES: Most certainly.

EUTHYPHRO: Who is it?

SOCRATES: I am not too clear about the man myself, Euthyphro. He appears to me to be a young man, and unknown. I think, however, that they call him Meletus, and his deme is Pitthos, if you happen to know anyone named Meletus of that deme—a hook-nosed man with long straight hair, and not much beard.

EUTHYPHRO: I don't recall him, Socrates. But tell c me, of what does he accuse you?

SOCRATES: His accusation? It is no mean charge. For a man of his age it is no small thing to have settled a question of so much importance. He says, in fact, that he knows the method by which young people are corrupted, and knows who the persons are that do it. He is, quite possibly, a wise man, and observing that my ignorance has led me to corrupt his generation, comes like a child to his mother to accuse me to the city. And to me he appears to be the only one who begins his po-
d litical activity aright, for the right way to begin is to pay attention to the young, and make them just as good as possible—precisely as the able farmer will give his attention to the young plants first, and afterward care for the rest. And so Meletus no doubt begins by clearing us away, the

ones who ruin, as he says, the tender shoots of 3
the young. That done, he obviously will care for
the older generation, and will thus become the
cause, in the highest and widest measure, of benefit to the state. With such a notable beginning,
his chances of success look good.

EUTHYPHRO: I hope so, Socrates, but I'm very
much afraid it will go the other way. When he
starts to injure you, it simply looks to me like beginning at the hearth to hurt the state. But tell
me what he says you do to corrupt the young.

SOCRATES: It sounds very queer, my friend, when b
first you hear it. He says I am a maker of gods;
he charges me with making new gods, and not
believing in the old ones. These are his grounds
for prosecuting me, he says.

EUTHYPHRO: I see it, Socrates. It is because you
say that ever and anon you have the spiritual sign!
So he charges you in this indictment with introducing novelties in religion, and that is the reason why he comes to court with this slanderous
complaint, well knowing how easily such matters
can be misrepresented to the crowd. For my own
part, when I speak in the Assembly about matters of religion, and tell them in advance what will c
occur, they laugh at me as if I were a madman,
and yet I never have made a prediction that did
not come true. But the truth is, they are jealous
of all such people as ourselves. No, we must not
worry over them, but go to meet them.

SOCRATES: Dear Euthyphro, if we were only
laughed at, it would be no serious matter. The

Athenians, as it seems to me, are not very much disturbed if they think that so-and-so is clever, so long as he does not impart his knowledge to anybody else. But the moment they suspect that he is giving his ability to others, they get angry, whether out of jealousy, as you say, or, it may be, for some other reason.

EUTHYPHRO: With regard to that, I am not very eager to test their attitude to me.

SOCRATES: Quite possibly you strike them as a man who is chary of himself, and is unwilling to impart his wisdom; as for me, I fear I am so kindly they will think that I pour out all I have to everyone, and not merely without pay—nay, rather, glad to offer something if it would induce someone to hear me. Well then, as I said just now, if they were going to laugh at me, as you say they do at you, it wouldn't be at all unpleasant to spend the time laughing and joking in court. But if they take the matter seriously, then there is no knowing how it will turn out. Only you prophets can tell!

EUTHYPHRO: Well, Socrates, perhaps no harm will come of it at all, but you will carry your case as you desire, and I think that I shall carry mine.

SOCRATES: Your case, Euthyphro? What is it? Are you prosecuting, or defending?

EUTHYPHRO: Prosecuting.

SOCRATES: Whom?

EUTHYPHRO: One whom I am thought a maniac to be attacking.

SOCRATES: How so? Is it someone who has wings to fly away with?

EUTHYPHRO: He is far from being able to do that; he happens to be old, a very old man.

SOCRATES: Who is it, then?

EUTHYPHRO: It is my father.

SOCRATES: Your father, my good friend?

EUTHYPHRO: Just so.

SOCRATES: What is the complaint? Of what do you accuse him?

EUTHYPHRO: Of murder, Socrates.

SOCRATES: Good heavens, Euthyphro! Surely the crowd is ignorant of the way things ought to go. I fancy it is not correct for any ordinary person to do that [to prosecute his father on this charge], but only for a man already far advanced in point of wisdom.

b

EUTHYPHRO: Yes, Socrates, by heaven! Far advanced!

SOCRATES: And the man your father killed, was he a relative of yours? Of course he was? You never would prosecute your father, would you, for the death of anybody who was not related to you?

EUTHYPHRO: You amuse me, Socrates. You think it makes a difference whether the victim was a member of the family, or not related, when the only thing to watch is whether it was right or not for the man who did the deed to kill him. If he

was justified, then let him go; if not, you have to
prosecute him, no matter if the man who killed
him shares your hearth, and sits at table with you.
The pollution is the same if, knowingly, you as-
sociate with such a man, and do not cleanse yourself, and him as well, by bringing him to justice.
The victim in this case was a laborer of mine, and
when we were cultivating land in Naxos, we em-
ployed him on our farm. One day he had been
drinking, and became enraged at one of our do-
mestics, and cut his throat; whereupon my father
bound him hand and foot, and threw him into a
ditch. Then he sent a man to Athens to find out
from the seer what ought to be done—meanwhile paying no attention to the man who had
been bound, neglecting him because he was a
murderer and it would be no great matter even
if he died. And that was just what happened.
Hunger, cold, and the shackles finished him before the messenger got back from visiting the
seer. That is why my father and my other kin are
bitter at me when I prosecute my father as a murderer. They say he did not kill the man, and had
he actually done it, the victim was himself a murderer, and for such a man one need have no consideration. They say that for a son to prosecute
his father as a murderer is unholy. How ill they
know divinity in its relation, Socrates, to what is
holy or unholy!

SOCRATES: But you, by heaven! Euthyphro, you
think that you have such an accurate knowledge
of things divine, and what is holy and unholy,

that, in circumstances such as you describe, you can accuse your father? You are not afraid that you yourself are doing an unholy deed?

EUTHYPHRO: Why, Socrates, if I did not have an 5
accurate knowledge of all that, I should be good for nothing, and Euthyphro would be no different from the general run of men.

SOCRATES: Well then, admirable Euthyphro, the best thing I can do is to become your pupil, and challenge Meletus before the trial comes on. Let me tell him that in the past I have considered it of great importance to know about things divine, and that now, when he asserts that I erroneously put forward my own notions and inventions on this head, I have become your pupil. I could say, Come, Meletus, if you agree that Euthyphro has wisdom in such matters, you must admit as well b
that I hold the true belief, and must not prosecute. If you do not, you must lodge your complaint, not against me, but against my aforesaid master; accuse him of corrupting the elder generation, me and his own father—me by his instruction, his father by correcting and chastising him.

And if he would not yield, would neither quit the suit nor yet indict you rather than myself, then I would say the same in court as when I challenged him!

EUTHYPHRO: Yes, Socrates, by heaven! If he undertook to bring me into court, I guess I would c
find out his rotten spot, and our talk there would

concern him sooner by a long shot than ever it would me!

SOCRATES: Yes, my dear friend, that I know, and so I wish to be your pupil. This Meletus, I perceive, along presumably with everybody else, appears to overlook you, but sees into me so easily and keenly that he has attacked me for impiety. So, in the name of heaven, tell me now about the matter you just felt sure you knew quite thoroughly. State what you take piety and impiety to be with reference to murder and all other cases.

d Is not the holy always one and the same thing in every action, and, again, is not the unholy always opposite to the holy, and like itself? And as unholiness does it not always have its one essential form, which will be found in everything that is unholy?

EUTHYPHRO: Yes, surely, Socrates.

SOCRATES: Then tell me. How do you define the holy and the unholy?

EUTHYPHRO: Well then, I say that the holy is what I am now doing, prosecuting the wrongdoer who commits a murder or a sacrilegious robbery, or sins in any point like that, whether it be your fa-

e ther, or your mother, or whoever it may be. And not to prosecute would be unholy. And, Socrates, observe what a decisive proof I will give you that such is the law. It is one I have already given to others; I tell them the right procedure must be not to tolerate the impious man, no matter who. Does not mankind believe that Zeus is the most excellent and just among the gods? And these

same men admit that Zeus shackled his own father [Cronus] for swallowing his [other] sons un-   6
justly, and that Cronus in turn had gelded his father [Uranus] for like reasons. But now they are
enraged at me when I proceed against my father
for wrongdoing, and so they contradict themselves in what they say about the gods and what
they say of me.

SOCRATES: There, Euthyphro, you have the reason why the charge is brought against me. It is
because, whenever people tell such stories about
the gods, I am prone to take it ill, and, so it
seems, that is why they will maintain that I am
sinful. Well, now, if you who are so well versed   b
in matters of the sort entertain the same beliefs,
then necessarily, it would seem, I must give in, for
what could we urge who admit that, for our own
part, we are quite ignorant about these matters?
But, in the name of friendship, tell me! Do you
actually believe that these things happened so?

EUTHYPHRO: Yes, Socrates, and things even more
amazing, of which the multitude does not know.

SOCRATES: And you actually believe that war occurred among the gods, and there were dreadful
hatreds, battles, and all sorts of fearful things like
that? Such things as the poets tell of, and good
artists represent in sacred places; yes, and at the
great Panathenaic festival the robe that is carried   c
up to the Acropolis is all inwrought with such
embellishments? What is our position, Euthyphro? Do we say that these things are true?

EUTHYPHRO: Not these things only, Socrates, but, as I just now said, I will, if you wish, relate to you many other stories about the gods, which I am certain will astonish you when you hear them.

SOCRATES: I shouldn't wonder. You shall tell me all about them when we have the leisure at some other time. At present try to tell me more clearly what I asked you a little while ago, for, my friend,
d   you were not explicit enough before when I put the question. What is holiness? You merely said that what you are now doing is a holy deed— namely, prosecuting your father on a charge of murder.

EUTHYPHRO: And, Socrates, I told the truth.

SOCRATES: Possibly. But, Euthyphro, there are many other things that you will say are holy.

EUTHYPHRO: Because they are.

SOCRATES: Well, bear in mind that what I asked of you was not to tell me one or two out of all the numerous actions that are holy; I wanted you to tell me what is the essential form of holiness which makes all holy actions holy. I believe you held that there is one ideal form by which un- holy things are all unholy, and by which all holy
e   things are holy. Do you remember that?

EUTHYPHRO: I do.

SOCRATES: Well then, show me what, precisely, this ideal is, so that, with my eye on it, and using it as a standard, I can say that any action done by you or anybody else is holy if it resembles this ideal, or, if it does not, can deny that it is holy.

EUTHYPHRO: Well, Socrates, if that is what you want, I certainly can tell you.

SOCRATES: It is precisely what I want.

EUTHYPHRO: Well then, what is pleasing to the gods is holy, and what is not pleasing to them is unholy. 7

SOCRATES: Perfect, Euthyphro! Now you give me just the answer that I asked for. Meanwhile, whether it is right I do not know, but obviously you will go on to prove your statement true.

EUTHYPHRO: Indeed I will.

SOCRATES: Come now, let us scrutinize what we are saying. What is pleasing to the gods, and the man that pleases them, are holy; what is hateful to the gods, and the man they hate, unholy. But the holy and unholy are not the same; the holy is directly opposite to the unholy. Isn't it so?

EUTHYPHRO: It is.

SOCRATES: And the matter clearly was well stated.

EUTHYPHRO: I accept it, Socrates; that was stated. b

SOCRATES: Was it not also stated, Euthyphro, that the gods revolt and differ with each other, and that hatreds come between them?

EUTHYPHRO: That was stated.

SOCRATES: Hatred and wrath, my friend—what kind of disagreement will produce them? Look at the matter thus. If you and I were to differ about numbers, on the question which of two was the greater, would a disagreement about that make

us angry at each other, and make enemies of us?
c Should we not settle things by calculation, and
so come to an agreement quickly on any point
like that?

EUTHYPHRO: Yes, certainly.

SOCRATES: And similarly if we differed on a question of greater length or less, we would take a measurement, and quickly put an end to the dispute?

EUTHYPHRO: Just that.

SOCRATES: And so, I fancy, we should have recourse to scales, and settle any question about a heavier or lighter weight?

EUTHYPHRO: Of course.

SOCRATES: What sort of thing, then, is it about which we differ, till, unable to arrive at a decision, we might get angry and be enemies to one an-
d other? Perhaps you have no answer ready, but listen to me. See if it is not the following—right and wrong, the noble and the base, and good and bad. Are not these the things about which we differ, till, unable to arrive at a decision, we grow hostile, when we do grow hostile, to each other, you and I and everybody else?

EUTHYPHRO: Yes, Socrates, that is where we differ, on these subjects.

SOCRATES: What about the gods, then, Euthyphro? If, indeed, they have dissensions, must it not be on these subjects?

EUTHYPHRO: Quite necessarily.

SOCRATES: Accordingly, my noble Euthyphro, by e
your account some gods take one thing to be
right, and others take another, and similarly with
the honorable and the base, and good and bad.
They would hardly be at variance with each
other, if they did not differ on these questions.
Would they?

EUTHYPHRO: You are right.

SOCRATES: And what each one of them thinks
noble, good, and just, is what he loves, and the
opposite is what he hates?

EUTHYPHRO: Yes, certainly.

SOCRATES: But it is the same things, so you say,
that some of them think right, and others wrong, 8
and through disputing about these they are at
variance, and make war on one another. Isn't it
so?

EUTHYPHRO: It is.

SOCRATES: Accordingly, so it would seem, the
same things will be hated by the gods and loved
by them; the same things would alike displease
and please them.

EUTHYPHRO: It would seem so.

SOCRATES: And so, according to this argument,
the same things, Euthyphro, will be holy and
unholy.

EUTHYPHRO: That may be.

SOCRATES: In that case, admirable friend, you
have not answered what I asked you. I did not ask

you to tell me what at once is holy and unholy, but it seems that what is pleasing to the gods is also hateful to them. Thus, Euthyphro, it would not be strange at all if what you now are doing in punishing your father were pleasing to Zeus, but hateful to Cronus and Uranus, and welcome to Hephaestus, but odious to Hera, and if any other of the gods disagree about the matter, satisfactory to some of them, and odious to others.

EUTHYPHRO: But, Socrates, my notion is that, on this point, there is no difference of opinion among the gods—not one of them but thinks that if a person kills another wrongfully, he ought to pay for it.

SOCRATES: And what of men? Have you never heard a man contending that someone who has killed a person wrongfully, or done some other unjust deed, ought not to pay the penalty?

EUTHYPHRO: Why! There is never any end to their disputes about these matters; it goes on everywhere, above all in the courts. People do all kinds of wrong, and then there is nothing they will not do or say in order to escape the penalty.

SOCRATES: Do they admit wrongdoing, Euthyphro, and, while admitting it, deny that they ought to pay the penalty?

EUTHYPHRO: No, not that, by any means.

SOCRATES: Then they will not do and say quite everything. Unless I am mistaken, they dare not say or argue that if they do wrong they should not pay the penalty. No, I think that they deny wrongdoing. How about it?   d

EUTHYPHRO: It is true.

SOCRATES: Therefore they do not dispute that anybody who does wrong should pay the penalty. No, the thing that they dispute about is likely to be who is the wrongdoer, what he did, and when.

EUTHYPHRO: That is true.

SOCRATES: Well then, isn't that precisely what goes on among the gods, if they really do have quarrels about right and wrong, as you say they do? One set will hold that some others do wrong, and the other set deny it? For that other thing, my friend, I take it no one, whether god or man, will dare to say—that the wrongdoer should not   e pay the penalty!

EUTHYPHRO: Yes, Socrates, what you say is true— in the main.

SOCRATES: It is the individual act, I fancy, Euthyphro, that the disputants dispute about, both men and gods, if gods ever do dispute. They differ on a certain act; some hold that it was rightly done, the others that it was wrong. Isn't it so?

EUTHYPHRO: Yes, certainly.

SOCRATES: Then come, dear Euthyphro, teach   9 me as well, and let me grow more wise. What proof have you that all the gods think that your servant died unjustly, your hireling, who, when he had killed a man, was shackled by the master of the victim, and perished, dying because of his shackles before the man who shackled him could learn from the seers what ought to be done with him? What proof have you that for a man like him it is right for a son to prosecute his father, and indict him on a charge of murder? Come on. Try to make it clear to me beyond all doubt that under these conditions the gods must all consider this action to be right. If you can adequately

b   prove it to me, I will never cease from praising you for your wisdom.

EUTHYPHRO: But, Socrates, that, very likely, would be no small task, although I could indeed make it very clear to you.

SOCRATES: I understand. You think that I am duller than the judges; obviously you will demonstrate to them that what your father did was wrong, and that the gods all hate such deeds.

EUTHYPHRO: I shall prove it absolutely, Socrates, if they will listen to me.

SOCRATES: They are sure to listen if they think

c   that you speak well. But while you were talking, a notion came into my head, and I asked myself, Suppose that Euthyphro proved to me quite clearly that all the gods consider such a death unjust; would I have come one whit the nearer for him to knowing what the holy is, and what the unholy? The act in question, seemingly, might be displeasing to the gods, but then we have just seen that you cannot define the holy and unholy in that way, for we have seen that a given thing may be displeasing, and also pleasing, to gods. So on this point, Euthyphro, I will let you off; if you like, the gods shall all consider the act unjust, and they all shall hate it. But suppose that we now correct our definition, and say what the gods all hate is unholy, and what they love is holy, whereas what some of them love, and others hate, is either both or neither. Are you willing that we now define the holy and unholy in this way?

d

EUTHYPHRO: What is there to prevent us, Socrates?

SOCRATES: Nothing to prevent me, Euthyphro. As for you, see whether when you take this definition you can quite readily instruct me, as you promised.

EUTHYPHRO: Yes, I would indeed affirm that holiness is what the gods all love, and its opposite is what the gods all hate, unholiness.

e

SOCRATES: Are we to examine this position also, Euthyphro, to see if it is sound? Or shall we let it through, and thus accept our own and others' statement, and agree to an assertion simply when somebody says that a thing is so? Must we not look into what the speaker says?

EUTHYPHRO: We must. And yet, for my part, I regard the present statement as correct.

SOCRATES: We shall soon know better about that, my friend. Now think of this. Is what is holy holy because the gods approve it, or do they approve it because it is holy?

10

EUTHYPHRO: I do not get your meaning.

1. The first line is the hidden key, as with most of Plato's dialogues. **"This, Socrates, is something new?"** (*Ti neoteron, O Sokrates*) is not a meaningless cliché ("What's new?" "¿Que pasa?") but signals the fact that Socrates is a radically new kind of man, and his enterprise, rational philosophy, is a radically new kind of enterprise. The Athenians who condemned him for atheism thought it was a new religion, but it was a new *kind* of religion, one that Euthyphro, a typical Athenian, simply does not understand.

2. The personal, dramatic contrast between the brash, *self*-righteous Euthyphro and the humble, righteous Socrates is as much a part of the dialogue as the contrast of ideas. Socrates philosophizes not only to find objective truth, like a scientist (he does that, too), but also as personal spiritual warfare (*jihad*), as an offer to heal darkened souls. Personal as well as logical demands are always made on his dialogue partner and on the reader. We are shown not only two philosophies between which to choose, but also two persons with whom to identify.

3. Socrates is the apostle of reason. He demands that we give logical reasons, grounds for beliefs, and follow the logical consequences of our beliefs, taken as premises or hypotheses, to their logical conclusions through a number of logically compelling steps. This is "Something new, Socrates". This had never been seen before in the history of mankind.

Yet Socrates' "new thing", care for logical consistency, does not exclude or destroy his instincts, his human affection, his piety, or his common sense. In fact, all those destructions happen in the soul of Euthyphro. Mere logical consistency drives Euthyphro to prosecute his own father for murder, because this is what a god once did. But Socrates is shocked at Euthyphro's lack of familial piety and loyalty. This shows something else besides reason working in Socrates. It is not pure reason that tells us to prefer our family, to be loyal to persons and not just to ideas or causes.[1] Socrates has not only reason but also piety (to both family and gods—these two pieties have usually gone together in history); Euthyphro thinks he has both but really has neither.

Thus, the contrast between Euthyphro and Socrates shows, by personal example, that reason and faith, logic and piety, philosophy and religion are natural allies, not enemies.

4. We see Plato's familiar irony in many places. First of all, in the situation. Socrates is about to be tried and executed for impiety, yet he shows his piety, in contrast with Euthyphro, who is about to secure his father's death out of his own impiety. Yet Euthyphro claims to know piety, and Socrates does not. All of Socrates' compliments to Euthyphro are ironic: his apparent praises are veiled insults: **"Only you prophets can tell"** (3e). **"Good heavens, Euthyphro! Surely the crowd is ignorant of the way things ought to go. I fancy it is not correct for any ordinary person to do that** [prosecute his own father] **but only for a man already far advanced in point of wisdom"** (4b). **"Admirable Euthyphro, the best thing I can do is to become your pupil"** (5a).

[1] There is a famous, purely rationalistic philosopher today, Peter Singer, who maintains that it is morally wrong to treat your own family in a special, preferential way because they are equal in value to strangers, according to a purely objective, logical consideration.

Piety is something defined as "holy fear", or "the fear of God". The Hebrew Scriptures call this "the beginning of wisdom" (Ps 111:10, Prov 9:10)—but not the end. Euthyphro has none of it, and Socrates has much: **"But you, by heaven! Euthyphro, you think that you have such an accurate knowledge of things divine, and what is holy and unholy, that, in circumstances such as you describe, you can accuse your father? You are not afraid that you yourself are doing an unholy deed?"** (4e).

Socrates will now seem to become the pupil of Euthyphro, the man who claims to know. Of course, behind the level of appearances, things are in reality exactly the ironic opposite: Socrates teaches Euthyphro something, while Euthyphro teaches Socrates nothing. Socrates teaches Euthyphro Lesson One, that he does not know, though Euthyphro does not learn it. But Euthyphro teaches Socrates nothing.

5. By imagining yourself in Euthyphro's position, you can easily understand why a city of Euthyphros would feel threatened by Socrates. People will often forgive you for being wrong where they are right; they will seldom forgive you for being right where they are wrong.

6. Socrates begins, as usual, by seeking a *definition* of the term *holiness* (5d). This is a necessary beginning because a term is the beginning of a proposition, and a proposition is the beginning of an argument. Therefore, if we do not know what we mean by a term, we simply will not know what we are talking about, no matter what we say in our propositions and our arguments.

A definition expresses the *essence* of the thing defined, the unchanging core, the one universal in all the different particular cases. As Socrates says, **"Is not the holy** [holiness, or piety] **always one and the same thing in every** [holy] **action, and, again, is not the unholy always opposite to the holy, and like itself? And as for unholiness does it not always have its one essential form** [nature, identity], **which will be found in everything that is unholy?"** (5d).

7. Euthyphro's first attempt at a definition is not universal but particular, a particular *example* of holiness rather than the universal *nature* of holiness: **"I say that the holy is what I am now doing"** (5d). This is like defining human nature by pointing to a human being. What is it that makes him, and all other human beings, human?

8. Euthyphro justifies his action in court as holy by appealing to the example of the gods: **"Zeus shackled his own father [Cronus] for swallowing his [other] sons unjustly and . . . Cronus in turn had gelded his father [Uranus] for like reasons"** (6a).

Socrates frankly admits that he does not believe these stories:

There, Euthyphro, you have the reason why the charge is brought against me. It is because whenever people tell such stories about the gods, I am prone to take it ill. . . . But, in the name of friendship, tell me! Do you actually believe that these things happened so? . . . And you actually believe that war occurred among the gods, and there were dreadful hatreds, battles, and all sorts of fearful things like that? (6ab)

Socrates tests the faith of the Athenians by reason and finds it wanting. We can see why they feared him: it is extremely troubling to alter your religious faith, and it may seem like betrayal to subject it to another standard, even that of reason and logical cross-examination.

9. Euthyphro finally gives a definition of holiness, after Socrates tells him the difference between a definition and an example: **"What I asked of you was not to tell me one or two out of all the numerous actions that are holy; I wanted you to tell me what is the essential form [nature] of holiness which makes all holy actions holy"** (6d). Euthyphro's definition is this: **"What is pleasing to the gods is holy, and what is not pleasing to them is unholy"** (7a).

Socrates praises Euthyphro for giving at last a definition. But is it a true one? **"Perfect, Euthyphro! Now you give me just the answer that I asked for. Meanwhile, whether it is right I do not know, but obviously [!] you will go on to prove your statement true"** (7a).

10. But it is quickly proved *untrue* because it contradicts what Euthyphro has assumed: that the gods differ from each other. For then what pleases one god would often displease another; so the same act would be both holy and unholy: a contradiction.

11. Euthyphro replies that *all* the gods agree that Euthyphro's father's deed was unjust. Socrates does not let himself be distracted from the main point, the essence of holiness, by arguing about what the gods think (a subject he claims to know nothing about), so he says, **"on this point, Euthyphro, I will let you off; if you like, the gods shall all consider the act**

unjust, and they all shall hate it. But suppose that we now correct our definition, and say what the gods all hate is unholy, and what they love is holy" (9d). At this point, the Jewish, Christian, or Muslim monotheist becomes as much involved as the pagan polytheist, for there is no longer a division of wills in divinity. The crucial question Socrates asks next is challenging not only to the polytheist but also to the monotheist, who would substitute "God" for "the gods".

12. "Is what is holy holy because the gods approve it, or do they approve it because it is holy?" (10a).

Euthyphro replies "I do not get your meaning" —and maybe you do not either.

Socrates explains, "Do you see what I wish to say, Euthyphro? It is this. Whenever an effect occurs, . . . there is a cause, and then comes this effect" (10c). The question Socrates asks Euthyphro is this: Which of these two—holiness or the approval of the gods—is the cause, and which is the effect? There are two possible answers:

(1) That the gods' approval (or "the will of God", for a monotheist) causes, that is, makes whatever they approve to be holy. If the gods approved cannibalism or genocide or egotism, that would be holy. "The holy" or "the pious" or "the good" is not anything in itself; it has no intrinsic nature; it is wholly relative to the gods' will.

(2) That the nature of holiness is unchangeable even by the gods. Their will is *made* holy by "the holy" (holiness) itself; even the gods are to be judged by a higher standard.

In (1), holiness is an effect of the gods' will; in (2)

the holiness of the gods' will is an effect of holiness in itself.

Euthyphro chooses (1) as his position. Socrates chooses (2). As long as "the gods" are the notoriously imperfect gods of Greece, it is clear that we have no contest. Euthyphro's position is shown to be irrational and self-contradictory. (The rather technical and very abstract argument Socrates uses is omitted here, since the religious belief of Euthyphro that Socrates refutes is not a live issue for most people today.)

But when we substitute the God of Abraham for the gods of Greece, we have a new problem. Position (1) makes God arbitrary, and position (2) makes God subject to a higher, independent standard. For (1), God is a tyrant; for (2), God is in the dock. For (1) God does what he condemns evil men for doing when he says: "Woe to those who call evil good and good evil" (Is 5:20). For (2), God has to look at the Ten Commandments on his wall every day to be sure he is being good.

Some Jews, Christians, and Muslims (but not all) do embrace a version of (1). Philosophers call it "the Divine Command theory". It amounts to the same answer a parent often gives to a child's question "Why should I?"—"Because I say so, that's why." Socrates would say that makes God a poor teacher.

The classic solution in Jewish, Christian, and Muslim theology is to deny Socrates' implicit assumption that holiness (or goodness or piety or virtue) and God's will are different and are related as cause and effect. Instead both "go all the way up". God's will is holiness. Holiness is God's own eternal nature, and God always wills in accordance with his nature.

(1)	(2)	(3)
God's will ↓ holiness, goodness	holiness, goodness ↓ God's will	God's will = holiness, goodness

13. The hidden issue here is the relation between religious faith and philosophical reason. We know what God or the gods will by faith, not reason. God must *reveal* his will, and we must accept this revelation by faith; we have no mental telepathy with the mind of God. But we can know the definition, essence, nature, form, or meaning of the concept of holiness by our own reason.

Thus Socrates, in holding that the gods will a thing because it is holy rather than it being holy because they will it, is ranking reason (which knows "the holy") above faith (which believes the gods). We know the gods better by reason than by faith. This poses problems for the Jew, Christian, or Muslim, who believes that God revealed to man many things human reason could not know, so that faith is a more complete knowledge of God than reason. (It is also more certain, for God can neither deceive nor be deceived, while man and his reason can.) But this presupposes a divine revelation; without it, Socrates is right.

The classic solution to this problem, given a divine revelation, is that both faith (when its object is truly divine revelation) and reason (when used correctly) can "go all the way up" and know some eternal truths about God and his nature; that they should cooperate and complete each other like a husband and wife or two wings of a bird.

The issue is complex, like a tree with many branches, and has been debated by millions of thinkers for thousands of years. But Socrates planted its seeds here.

14. Each time Euthyphro tries to give an answer to Socrates' questions, the answer turns out to contradict itself or something else Euthyphro says. Euthyphro runs various flags up his flagpole, but he cannot get Socrates to salute any one of them. This must have been embarrassing and frustrating—and very surprising to someone like Euthyphro, who felt so certain that he was an expert on holiness. Socrates repeatedly encourages him to try again, but Euthyphro eventually gives up:

> **Consequently, Euthyphro, it looks as if you had not given me my answer—as if when you were asked to tell the nature of the holy, you did not wish to explain the essence of it. You merely tell an attribute of it, namely, that it appertains to holiness to be loved by all the gods. What it *is*, as yet you have not said. So, if you please, do not conceal this from me. No, begin again.** (11a)

> **And so we must go back again, and start from the beginning to find out what the holy is. As for me, I will never give up until I know. Ah! Do not spurn me, but give me your mind with all your might now at length to tell me the absolute truth, for if anybody knows, of all mankind, it is you. . . . If you did not know precisely what is holy and unholy, it is unthinkable that . . . you ever would have moved to prosecute your aged sire on a charge of**

murder. No, you would have feared to risk the wrath of the gods on the chance that you were not doing right, and would have been afraid of the talk of men. But now I am sure that you think you know exactly what is holy and what is not. So tell me, peerless Euthyphro, and do not hide from me what you judge it to be.

EUTHYPHRO: Another time, Socrates, for I am in a hurry, and must be off this minute. (15de)

Will you be like Euthyphro? Or will you be like Socrates?

15. The question of God or the gods is the question about the greatest being(s), the greatest reality; so it is the greatest question, whatever the answer is.

It is not a scientific question, for the scientific method is limited to the sensible and measurable—though some scientific evidence is relevant to it, such as the Big Bang or evolution.

It is not a historical question, for God is not an entity in time and history, though some historical evidence is relevant to it, such as prophets, miracles, the claims of Jesus, and the lives of believers.

It is a philosophical question, a question about wisdom. Is it wise or unwise to believe we have an invisible Creator and Lord? That our lives are parts of a divinely known story? Is it childish foolishness, "fairy-tale thinking", or is it mature wisdom?

16. The most practically important aspect of the God question is the one raised in the *Euthyphro*, the connection between God and moral goodness. Do we need God to be good? Does a universal moral law

prove a universal moral lawgiver? Without God, are all things permissible?

Some, like Euthyphro and Dostoyevski, say Yes: Without a real God there is no real goodness, and both *are* real. Others, like Nietzsche and Sartre, say Yes to the connection (God and morality sink or swim together) but No to both parts: There is no God and, therefore, no real good. Still others, like Socrates, deny the connection but believe in both God and goodness. Still others (humanists) deny the connection and believe in goodness but not God.

The atheist's reaction to the *Euthyphro* would be: "See? Socrates shows how illogical religion is and how destructive it is to pin morality to God." The theist's reaction to the same dialogue would be: "See? Socrates purifies the notion of God *and* the notion of goodness or piety." The agnostic's reaction would be: "Socrates' God is 'the unknown God' of Acts 17, and he must remain unknown, if we are honest and humble like Socrates. About God, God only knows."

The religious Jew, Christian, or Muslim would add that the agnostic may be right, but God has come out of hiding, so to speak, and revealed himself, so that we, too, can know what God only knows. And this goes beyond Socrates. Whether Socrates would have the same negative critique of the God half the world now worships as he had of the gods of Euthyphro is a fascinating question. And the answer to it, God only knows.[2]

---

[2] However, we may speculate and imagine, as I did in *Socrates Meets Jesus*, in which Socrates is reincarnated as a student at Harvard Divinity School and asks his teachers and fellow students surprising and uncomfortable questions.

III

From the *Phaedo*:
Philosophy Martyred

ECHECRATES: Were you there yourself, Phaidon,
with Socrates, on the day when he took the poison in prison, or did you hear about it from
someone?

PHAIDON: I was there myself, Echecrates.

ECHECRATES: Then what was it our friend said
before his death? And how did he end? I should
be glad to hear. You see no one at all from our
part of the world goes now to visit in Athens, and
no visitor has come to us from there this long
time who might be able to tell us properly what   b
happened; all they could say was, he took the poison and died; no one could tell us anything about
the other details.

PHAIDON: Then you never heard how things went   58
at the trial?

ECHECRATES: Yes, somebody did bring news of
that, and we were surprised how long it seemed
between the sentence and his death. Why was
that, Phaidon?

PHAIDON: It was just a piece of luck, Echecrates;
for the day before the trial it so happened that
the wreath was put on the poop of the ship which
the Athenians send to Delos.

ECHECRATES: What ship is that?

PHAIDON: That is the ship, as the Athenians say, in which Theseus once went off to Crete with those "twice seven," you know, and saved them b and saved himself. The Athenians vowed to Apollo then, so it is said, that if the lives of these were saved, they would send a sacred mission every year to Delos; and they do send it still, every year ever since that, to honour the god. As soon as the mission has begun, then, it is their law to keep the city pure during that time, and to put no one to death before the ship arrives at Delos and comes back again here; this often takes c some time, when the winds happen to delay them. The beginning of the mission is when the priest of Apollo lays a wreath on the poop of the ship, and this happened, as I say, the day before the trial. Accordingly Socrates had a long time in prison between the trial and his death.

ECHECRATES: Then what about the death itself, Phaidon? What was said or done, and which of his friends were with him? Or did the magistrates forbid their presence, and did he die alone with no friends there?

d PHAIDON: Oh no, friends were with him, quite a number of them.

ECHECRATES: That's just what I want to know; please be so kind as to tell me all about it as clearly as possible, unless you happen to be busy.

PHAIDON: Oh, I have plenty of time, and I will try to tell you the whole story; indeed, to remember

Socrates, and what he said himself, and what was said to him is always the most precious thing in the world to me.

ECHECRATES: Well, Phaidon, those who are going to hear you will feel the same; pray try to tell the whole story as exactly as you can.

PHAIDON: I must say I had the strangest feeling   e
being there. I felt no pity, as one might, being present at the death of a dear friend; for the man seemed happy to me, Echecrates, in bearing and in speech. How fearlessly and nobly he met his end! I could not help thinking that divine providence was with that man as he passed from this world to the next, and on coming there also it would be well with him, if ever with anyone that ever was. For this reason I felt no pity at all, as   59
one might at a scene of mourning; and yet not the pleasure we used to have in our philosophic discussions. The conversation was certainly of that sort, but I really had an extraordinary feeling, a strange mixture of pleasure and pain at once, when I remembered that then and there that man was to make his end. And all of us who were present were very much in the same state, sometimes laughing, sometimes shedding tears, and one of us particularly, Apollodoros—no doubt you know   b
the man and his ways.

ECHECRATES: Oh yes, of course.

PHAIDON: Well, he behaved quite as usual, and I was broken down myself, and so were others.

ECHECRATES: But who were they, Phaidon?

PHAIDON: Of our countrymen there was this Apollodoros I have mentioned, and Critobulos and his father, and besides, Hermogenes and Epigenes and Aischines and Antisthenes; there was also Ctesippos the Paianian and Menexenos, and others of our countrymen; but Plato was ill, I think.

ECHECRATES: Were any foreigners present?

c   PHAIDON: Yes, Simmias the Theban and Cebes and Phaidondes; and from Megara, Eucleides and Terpsion.

ECHECRATES: Oh, were not Aristippos and Cleombrotos present?

PHAIDON: No, they were said to be in Aegina.

ECHECRATES: Was anyone else there?

PHAIDON: I think these are about all who were present.

ECHECRATES: Very well; tell me, what did you talk about?

PHAIDON: I will try to tell you the whole story
d   from the beginning. You see we had been accustomed during all the former days to visit Socrates, myself and the rest. We used to gather early at the court where the trial had been, for that was near the prison. We always waited until the prison was opened, passing the time together, for it was not opened early; and when it was opened we went in to Socrates and generally spent the day with him. That day, however, we gathered earlier than usual; for the day before, after we left the

prison in the evening, we learnt that the ship had   e
come in from Delos; so we warned one another
to come as early as possible to the usual place.
We came early, then, and the porter who used
to answer the door came out to us, and told us
to wait and not to go in till he gave the word;
for, he said, "The Eleven are knocking off his
fetters and informing him that he must die today."

After a short while he came back and told us
to go in. So we went in, and found Socrates just   60
released, and Xanthippe, you know her, with his
little boy, sitting beside him. Then when Xanthippe saw us, she cried out in lamentation and
said as women do, "O Socrates! Here is the last
time your friends will speak to you and you to
them!"

Socrates glanced at Criton and said quietly,
"Please let someone take her home, Criton."

Then some of Criton's people led her away cry-
ing and beating her breast. Socrates sat up on his
bed, and bent back his leg and rubbed it with his
hand, and said while he rubbed it, "How strange   b
a thing it seems, my friends, that which people
call pleasure! And how wonderful is its relation
to pain, which they suppose to be its opposite;
both together they will not come to a man, yet if
he pursues one of the pair, and catches it, he is
almost compelled to catch the other, too; so they
seem to be both hung together from one head. I
think that Aesop would have made a fable, if he   c
had noticed this; he would have said they were at
war, and God wanted to make peace between
them and could not, and accordingly hung them

together by their heads to the same thing, and therefore whenever you get one, the other follows after. That's just what it seems like to me; first came the pain in my leg from the irons, and here seems to come following it, pleasure."

Cebes took up here, and said, "Upon my word, Socrates, I am much obliged to you for reminding me. About your poems, I mean, when you put into verse Aesop's fables, and the prelude for d Apollo; many people have asked me, for example Euenos, the other day, what on earth put it in your mind to make those poems after you came into prison, although you never made any before. Then if you care that I should be able to answer Euenos, next time he asks me, and I'm sure he will, tell me what to say."

"Tell him then, Cebes," he said, "just the truth: e that I did not want to rival him or his creations when I did it, for I knew it would not be easy; but I was trying to find out the meaning of certain dreams, and getting it off my conscience, in case they meant to command me to attempt that sort of composition. The dreams went like this: In my past life, the same dream often used to come to me, in different shapes at different times, but saying the same thing, 'Socrates, get to work and compose music!' Formerly I took this to mean what I was already doing; I thought the dream was urging and encouraging me, as people do in cheering on their own men when they are running a race, to compose—which, taking 61 philosophy to be the highest form of composition, I was doing already; but now after the trial, while the festival was putting off my execution, I

thought that, if the dream should really command me to work at this common kind of composition, I ought not to disobey the dream but
to do so. For it seemed safer not to go away before getting it off my conscience by composing
poetry, and so obeying the dream. So first of all   b
I composed in honour of the god whose festival
this was; after the god, I considered that a poet
must compose fiction if he was to be a poet, not
true tales, and I was no fiction-monger, and
therefore I took the fictions that I found to my
hand and knew, namely Aesop's, and composed
the first that came. Then tell Euenos that, Cebes,
and bid him farewell, and tell him to follow me
as soon as he can, if he is sensible. I am going
away, as it seems, today; for so the Athenians   c
command."

"What advice, Socrates," he said, "to give to
Euenos! I have often met the man; from what I
have seen of him so far he will be the last man to
obey!"

"Why," said he, "is not Euenos a philosopher?"

"I think so," said Simmias.

"Then Euenos will be willing enough, and so
will everyone who goes properly into the subject.
But perhaps he will not do violence to himself;
for they say that is not lawful."

As he spoke, he let down his legs on to the
ground, and sat thus during the rest of the talk.   d
Then Cebes asked him, "What do you mean,
Socrates, by saying, that it is not lawful for a man
to do violence to himself, but that the philosopher would be willing to follow the dying?"

"Why, Cebes," he said, "have not you and Sim-

mias heard all about such things from Philolaos,
when you were his pupils?"

"Nothing clear, Socrates."

"Well truly, all I say myself is only from hear-
say; however, what I happen to have heard I don't
mind telling you. Indeed, it is perhaps most
e   proper that one who is going to depart and take
up his abode in that world should think about the
life over there and say what sort of life we imagine it to be: for what else could one do with the
time till sunset?"

"Well then, why pray do they say it is not lawful for a man to take his own life, my dear Socrates? I have already heard Philolaos myself, as
you asked me just now, when he was staying in
our parts, and I have heard others too, and they
all said we must not do that; but I never heard
anything clear about it."

62   "Well, go on trying," said Socrates, "and perhaps you may hear something. It might perhaps
seem surprising to you if in this one thing, of all
that happens to a human being, there is never any
exception—if it never chances to a man amongst
the other chances of his life that sometimes for
some people it is better to die than to live; but it
does probably seem surprising to you if those
people for whom it *is* better to die may not
rightly do this good to themselves, but must wait
for some other benefactor."

And Cebes answered, with a light laugh. "True
for ye, by Zeus!" using his native Doric.

b   "Indeed, put like this," said Socrates, "it would
seem unreasonable; but possibly there is a grain
of reason in it. At least, the tale whispered in se-

cret about these things is that we men are in a
sort of custody, and a man must not release himself or run away, which appears a great mystery
to me and not easy to see through. But I do think,
Cebes, it is right to say the gods are those who
take care of us, and that we men are one of the
gods' possessions—don't you think so?"

"Yes, I do," said Cebes.

"Then," said he, "if one of your own posses-   c
sions, your slave, should kill himself, without your
indicating to him that you wanted him to die, you
would be angry with him, and punish him if there
were any punishment?"

"Certainly," said he.

"Possibly, then, it is not unreasonable in that
sense, that a man must not kill himself before
God sends on him some necessity, like that which
is present here now."

"Yes indeed, that seems likely," said Cebes.
"But you said just now, Socrates, that philosophers ought cheerfully to be willing to die; that
does seem unreasonable, at least if there is reason in what we have just said, that God is he who
cares for us and we are his possessions. That the   d
wisest men should not object to depart out of this
service in which we are overseen by the best over-
seers there are, gods, there is no reason in that.
For I don't suppose a wise man thinks he will care
better for himself when he is free. But a foolish
man might well believe that he should run away
from an owner; and he would not remember that   e
from a good one he ought not to run away but
to stay as long as he could, and so he would
thoughtlessly run away, while the man of sense

would desire always to be with one better than
himself. Indeed, in this case, Socrates, the opposite of what was said would be likely: It is proper
that wise men should object to die, and foolish
men should be glad."

63   Socrates, hearing this, was pleased, I thought,
at the way Cebes dealt with the matter; and,
glancing away at us, he said, "Cebes is always
on the hunt for arguments, and won't believe
straight off whatever one says."

And Simmias added, "But I tell you, Socrates,
I think I now see something in what Cebes says,
myself; for what could men want, if they are truly
wise, in running away from owners better than
themselves, and lightly shaking them off? And I
really think Cebes is aiming his argument at you,
because you take it so easily to leave both us and
good masters, as you admit yourself, gods!"

b   "Quite right," said he. "I think I must answer
this before you just as if you were a court!"

"Exactly," said Simmias.

"Very well," said he, "I will try to convince you
better than I did my judges. . . ."

[Most of the *Phaedo* is omitted here, and summarized
on pp. 139–42 (points 9 and 10). We add only the
last scene, Socrates' death.

After speculating about the details of the next life,
Socrates says:]

[114]d   "No sensible man would think it proper to rely
on things of this kind being just as I have described; but that, since the soul is clearly immortal, this or something like this at any rate is
what happens in regard to our souls and their

habitations—that this is so seems to me proper and worthy of the risk of believing; for the risk is noble. Such things he must sing like a healing charm to himself. and that is why I have lingered so long over the story. But these are the reasons e for a man to be confident about his own soul, when in his life he has bidden farewell to all other pleasures, the pleasures and adornments of the body, thinking them alien and such as do more harm than good, and has been earnest only for the pleasure of learning; and having adorned the soul with no alien ornaments, but with her own— with temperance and justice and courage and freedom and truth, thus he awaits the journey to the house of Hades, ready to travel when the doom ordained shall call. You indeed," he said, 115 "Simmias and Cebes and all, hereafter at some certain time shall each travel on that journey: but me—'Fate calls me now,' as a man might say in a tragedy, and it is almost time for me to travel towards the bath; for I am sure you think it better to have a bath before drinking the potion, and to save the women the trouble of washing a corpse."

When he had spoken, Criton said, "Ah well, b Socrates, what injunctions have you for these friends or for me, about your children or anything else? What could we do for you to gratify you most?"

"What I always say, Criton," he said, "nothing very new: Take good care of yourselves, and you will gratify me and mine and yourselves whatever you do, even if you promise nothing now. But if you neglect yourselves, and won't take care to live your lives following the footsteps, so to speak, of both this last conversation and those we have had in former times, you will do no good even if you promise ever so much at present and ever so faithfully."

c   "Then we will do our best about that," he said; "but how are we to bury you?"

"How you like," said he, "if you catch me and I don't escape you." At the same time, laughing gently and looking towards us, he said, "Criton doesn't believe me, my friends, that this is I, Socrates now talking with you and laying down each of my injunctions, but he thinks me to be what he will see shortly, a corpse, and asks, if you please, how to bury me! I have been saying all this

d long time, that when I have drunk the potion, I shall not be here then with you; I shall have gone clear away to some bliss of the blest, as they call it. But he thinks I am talking nonsense, just to console myself, yes and you too. Then go bail for me to Criton," he said, "the opposite of the bail he gave to those judges. He gave bail that I would remain; you please, give bail that I will not remain after I die, but I shall get off clear and clean, that Criton may take it more easily, and may not be

e vexed by seeing my body either being burnt or buried; don't let him worry for me and think I'm in a dreadful state, or say at the funeral that he is laying out or carrying out or digging in Socrates. Be sure, Criton, best of friends," he said, "to use ugly words not only is out of tune with the event, but it even infects the soul with something evil. Now, be confident and say you are burying my body, and then bury it as you please and as you think would be most according to custom."

With these words, he got up and retired into 116
another room for the bath, and Criton went after him, telling us to wait. So we waited discussing and talking together about what had been said, or sometimes speaking of the great misfortune which had befallen us, for we felt really as if we had lost a father and had to spend the rest of our lives as orphans. When he had bathed, and his children had been brought to see him—for he had two little sons, and one big—and b
when the women of his family had come, he talked to them before Criton and gave what instructions he wished. Then he asked the women and children to go, and came back to us. It was now near sunset, for he had spent a long time within. He came and sat down after his bath, and he had not talked long after this when the servant of the Eleven came in, and standing by him said, "O Socrates! I have not to complain of you c
as I do of others, that they are angry with me, and curse me, because I bring them word to drink their potion, which my officers make me do! But I have always found you in this time most generous and gentle, and the best man who ever came here. And now too, I know well you are not angry with me, for you know who are responsible, and you keep it for them. Now you know what I came to tell you, so farewell, and try to bear as well as you can what can't be helped."

Then he turned and was going out, with tears d
running down his cheeks. And Socrates looked up

at him and said, "Farewell to you also, I will do so." Then, at the same time turning to us, "What a nice fellow!" he said. "All the time he has been coming and talking to me, a real good sort, and now how generously he sheds tears for me! Come along, Criton, let's obey him. Someone bring the potion, if the stuff has been ground; if not, let the fellow grind it."

e   Then Criton said, "But, Socrates, I think the sun is still over the hills, it has not set yet. Yes, and I know of others who, having been told to drink the poison, have done it very late; they had dinner first and a good one, and some enjoyed the company of any they wanted. Please don't be in a hurry, there is time to spare."

But Socrates said, "Those you speak of have very good reason for doing that, for they think they will gain by doing it; and I have good reasons why I won't do it. For I think I shall gain 117   nothing by drinking a little later, only that I shall think myself a fool for clinging to life and sparing when the cask's empty. Come along," he said, "do what I tell you, if you please."

And Criton, hearing this, nodded to the boy who stood near. The boy went out, and after spending a long time, came in with the man who was to give the poison carrying it ground ready in a cup. Socrates caught sight of the man and said, "Here, my good man, you know about these things; what must I do?"

b   "Just drink it," he said, "and walk about till your legs get heavy, then lie down. In that way the drug will act of itself."

At the same time, he held out the cup to Socrates, and he took it quite cheerfully, Echecrates, not a tremble, not a change in colour or looks; but looking full at the man under his brows, as he used to do, he asked him. "What do you say about this drink? What of a libation to someone? Is that allowed, or not?"

He said, "We only grind so much as we think enough for a moderate potion."

"I understand," he said, "but at least, I suppose, c it is allowed to offer a prayer to the gods and that must be done, for good luck in the migration from here to there. Then that is my prayer, and so may it be!"

With these words he put the cup to his lips and, quite easy and contented, drank it up. So far most of us had been able to hold back our tears pretty well; but when we saw him begin drinking and end drinking, we could no longer. I burst into a flood of tears for all I could do, so I wrapped up my face and cried myself out; not for him indeed, but for my own misfortune in losing such a man and such a comrade. Criton had got d up and gone out even before I did, for he could not hold the tears in. Apollodoros had never ceased weeping all this time, and now he burst out into loud sobs, and by his weeping and lamentations completely broke down every man there except Socrates himself. He only said, "What a scene! You amaze me. That's just why I sent the women away, to keep them from making a scene like this. I've heard that one ought to make an end in decent silence. Quiet yourselves and endure." e

When we heard him we felt ashamed and restrained our tears. He walked about, and when he said that his legs were feeling heavy, he lay down on his back, as the man told him to do; at the same time the one who gave him the potion felt him, and after a while examined his feet and legs; then pinching a foot hard, he asked if he felt any-118   thing; he said no. After this, again, he pressed the shins; and moving up like this, he showed us that he was growing cold and stiff. Again he felt him, and told us that when it came to his heart, he would be gone. Already the cold had come nearly as far as the abdomen, when Socrates threw off the covering from his face—for he had covered it over—and said, the last words he uttered, "Criton," he said, "we owe a cock to Asclepios; pay it without fail."

"That indeed shall be done," said Criton. "Have you anything more to say?"

When Criton had asked this, Socrates gave no further answer, but after a little time, he stirred, and the man uncovered him, and his eyes were still. Criton, seeing this, closed the mouth and eyelids.

This was the end of our comrade, Echecrates, a man, as we would say, of all then living we had ever met, the noblest and the wisest and most just.

1. The *Phaedo* is an account of the death of Socrates. This is *not* the death of philosophy, but rather its life, its ongoing liveliness in the hands of Plato, Socrates' "apostle".

Like the *Apology*, it has two dimensions: the personal, particular, psychological picture of Socrates and the objective, universal, timeless picture of philosophy that Socrates exemplifies. No one else can ever be Socrates, but anyone can and should be philosophical. The excerpts given here, the dialogue's beginning and end, focus on the person of Socrates. But this cannot be divorced from the nature of philosophy. Socrates incarnates philosophy; he is its archetype, so that one could say that in a sense Socrates *is* philosophy, and philosophy is Socrates.

This is why it is not important whether all the details of Plato's accounts of Socrates are historically factual or not. Like Adam, Gilgamesh, Job, Confucius, Lao-tzu, Buddha, Ulysses, Caesar, and King Arthur, he is an icon, an archetype, an ideal. He is "larger than life".

It would destroy the faith of a religious Jew to discover that Moses never existed, or that he did not really receive the law from God. It would destroy the faith of an orthodox Christian to discover the bones of Jesus in a Jerusalem tomb. It would destroy the faith of a Muslim to believe that Muhammad invented the Qur'an rather than received it from Allah. But even if historians should prove that Socrates was only Plato's invention, philosophy would not die with the death of the historical Socrates, any more than Buddhist "enlightenment" would die with the debunking of the historical Buddha. Moses, Jesus, and Muhammad are prophets.[1] A prophet is unique and irreplaceable. No one can step into those

---

[1] I do not mean to assume that they are all true prophets, only that they claim to be. Nor do I mean to assume that Jesus is or is not something more than a prophet, as he claims to be. A prophet transmits wisdom; a philosopher seeks it; a sophist fakes it; God has it.

shoes on his own initiative. A prophet is made by God and authorized by God. But a philosopher is simply anyone who seeks wisdom, using human reason. Anyone and everyone is invited to step into Socrates' shoes (or footsteps: he was usually barefoot), and to do so on his own initiative, his own responsibility, his own free choice.

2. The first line, as it usually does in a Platonic dialogue, gives a hidden clue to the dialogue's deepest, central point. Years after Socrates' death, one of his disciples (Echecrates) asks another (Phaedo), **"Were you there yourself, Phaidon, with Socrates, on the day he took the poison in prison, or did you hear about it from someone?"**

The reader is tested here. **"Were you there yourself?"** Of course we were not; we were born thousands of years too late. But we *can* be there in spirit, for the spirit transcends the laws of matter and body. We can "identify with", that is, find our identity in, Jesus or Socrates or both. Just as there are two ways to read the Gospels—from without, as an observer, or from within, as a disciple—so there are these two ways to read the *Phaedo*. And Plato is here inviting us to read it in the same spirit in which he wrote it (which, by the way, is the first principle of good literary criticism and interpretation). Plato himself was absent in body since he was ill (9c). But he was "there" in spirit. And we can be there, too.

The difference between "being there yourself" (firsthand) and "hearing about it from someone" is sharply shown in the Book of Job. Job, the man from Missouri ("show me"), is not satisfied with any of his friends' secondhand knowledge of God but only with receiving the firsthand knowledge that moves him to say to God, at the story's climax, "I had heard of you [secondhand] by the hearing of the ear, but now my eye sees you" (Job 42:4).

3. After Phaedo replies, **"I was there myself, Echecrates"**, Echecrates asks two questions: **"Then what was it our friend said before his death? And how did he end?"** The *Phaedo* is divided into these two parts, Socrates' words and his deeds. The words, the arguments of Socrates to try to prove the immortality of the soul to his doubtful disciples, take up most of the dialogue, the middle section. They are omitted here because the most impressive "argument" for immortality is Socrates' example, his philosophy lived rather than verbalized. Few skeptics have been convinced to change their mind about immortality simply by Socrates' arguments (summarized below, point 8), but everyone is deeply moved and impressed by the actual death of Socrates, at the end of the *Phaedo*. It is one of the greatest passages in the world's literature. And it is, in a deep and mysterious way, quite convincing.

When C. S. Lewis' admired friend Charles Williams died, Lewis wrote this epitaph: "No event has so corroborated my belief in the afterlife as Williams did simply by dying. For when the idea of death and the idea of Charles Williams thus met in my mind, it was the idea of death that was changed." Plato says exactly the same thing about Socrates in the *Phaedo*.

4. Socrates' execution was delayed by the voyage of a sacred ship. Phaedo explains,

the ship which the Athenians send to Delos [the site of the Delphic oracle] **... is the ship, as the Athenians say, in which Theseus once**

**went off to Crete with those "twice seven,"
you know, and saved them and saved himself.
The Athenians vowed to Apollo then, so it is
said, that if the lives of these were saved, they
would send a sacred mission every year to
Delos; and they do send it still, every year
since that, to honour the god. As soon as the
mission has begun, then, it is their law to
keep the city pure during that time, and to
put no one to death before the ship arrives.**
(58ab)

According to the legend, Theseus of Athens went
to Crete and killed the monster Minotaur, and
Athens atoned for her past misdeeds by sending seven
boys and seven girls to King Minos of Crete every
ninth year to fight the Minotaur ritually in an ath-
letic liturgical dance. Plato is probably implying that
here Socrates fulfills the Theseus myth, as he fulfills
other myths (see page 69), by saving the barbarians
(us!) from the monsters within us.

The fourteen dancers were physically very much
unlike Socrates. They were young, beautiful, lithe,
and quick; he was old, ugly, fat, and slow. But his
spirit, his soul, his mind was exactly like these
sprightly young bullfighter dancers—a perfect sym-
bol of Socrates' wit and method. It is also a fitting
example of the Socratic contrast between visible appearance and invisible reality.

Jesus, too, was executed at the border of a sacred
time, the Jewish Sabbath, when the law forbade any
part of a killing; that is why they had to be sure he
was dead, and take down his body, before sunset on
Friday, when the Sabbath began (Jn 19:30–37).

The sacred ship from Athens brought the finest of Athenian youth as a tribute to the god of the Delphic oracle. Socrates was really Athens' finest, and when the ship docks, he is offered up for his loyalty to this same god.

The sacred ship also brings a return blessing to Athens from the god. This Socrates also was—a blessing on Athens, a gift from the god.

And Socrates himself gets a gift from the god when "his ship comes in". The gift is death, his ticket to heaven.

5. Phaedo says (at 58d) **"to remember Socrates, and what he said himself, and what was said to him is always the most precious thing in the world to me."** It was that to Plato, but this "remembering" was not an ending but a beginning, a stimulus to new philosophizing. For the spirit of Socrates is an active one, not a passive one. In a real sense, Socrates can have no disciples, for he has almost nothing to teach except his method, which we must practice ourselves, in action.

In this sense all philosophy is "remembering" Socrates, recapitulating him, making his "thing" actually present. It is almost sacramental ("Do this in remembrance of me.") It is almost a "real presence". It is certainly more like that than like a photograph.

6. In Socrates' presence common categories shift, and distinctions that we have assumed to be clear become unclear. And yet this new confusion is not a departure from, but exactly matches, our experience. One example of this concerns the relation between pleasure and pain. This is mentioned by both Phaedo and, soon after, by Socrates: **"I must say I had the strangest feeling being there. I felt no pity, as one**

might, being present at the death of a dear friend; for the man seemed happy to me. . . . I really had an extraordinary feeling, a strange mixture of pleasure and pain at once" (58e).

A little later, Socrates sat up on his bed, and bent back his leg and rubbed it with his hand, and said while he rubbed it, "How strange a thing it seems, my friends, that which people call pleasure! And how wonderful is its relation to pain, which they suppose to be its opposite; both together they will not come to a man; yet if he pursues one of the pair, and catches it, he is almost compelled to catch the other, too. . . . First came the pain in my leg from the irons, and here seems to come following after it, pleasure. (60bc)

The Socratic method questions our categories (for example, pleasure and pain) and our assumptions (for example, that they are exclusive of each other), but it does not question the data of our experience. Like the "scientific method", it tests hypotheses by the data rather than by ignoring or skewing the data for the sake of preserving hypotheses. The only difference between the two methods is that science narrows both its data and its hypotheses to the empirically verifiable or falsifiable (and, in the exact sciences, to the quantitatively measurable). But in both methods, the experience tests the idea and the data controls the hypothesis. That is one part of the logic of both methods, the inductive half. The deductive half calculates logical consequences from hypotheses. (In science this is usually prediction.)

7. What did Socrates do in prison on the last night of his life? Two things he had never done before: he wrote poems and a hymn:

> **"About your poems ... you put into verse Aesop's fables, and the prelude for Apollo; ... what on earth put it in your mind to make those poems after you came into prison, although you never made any before...."**
>
> **"... I was trying to find out the meaning of certain dreams.... 'Socrates, get to work and compose music!' Formerly I took this to mean what I was already doing; ... taking philosophy to be the highest form of composition ... ; but now, ... I thought that if the dream should really command me to work at this common kind of composition, I ought not to disobey the dream but to do so. For it seemed safer not to go away before getting it off my conscience by composing poetry, and so obeying the dream. So first of all I composed in honour of the god [Apollo] whose festival this was; after the god, I considered that a poet must compose fiction ... and I was no fiction-monger, and therefore I took the fictions that I knew, namely Aesop's." (60d–61b)**

Socrates, remember, is wise because he does not think he knows that which he does not know. All his life he *believed* the dream commanded him to "make music" not literally but symbolically, philosophy being the highest kind of music: the harmony and beauty of the highest part of the soul, the intellect. But perhaps he was wrong. If so, and if the dream came from the god, he has only one last chance to be pious and obey it.

Apollo and Aesop are the two most fitting choices for Socrates. Of all the gods, Apollo was the closest to what Socrates believed, for as the god of the sun, Apollo naturally symbolized reason and enlightenment and truth. Of all the poets, Aesop, author of fables about talking animals for children, is closest to Socrates because of his humility (he wrote for children), his morality (each fable teaches a moral lesson), and his truthfulness (no one mistook his tales for literal fact).

8. Cebes asks Socrates a question that many in our culture are confused about: If death is good, not evil, why is suicide evil, not good? (**"What do you mean, Socrates, by saying, that it is not lawful for a man to do violence to himself, but that the philosopher would be willing to follow the dying?"** [62c]).

Socrates responds not with a *logos*, or proof but with a *mythos*, or "sacred story" that he finds believable: **"Indeed, put like this, . . . it would seem unreasonable; but possibly there is a grain of reason in it. At least, the tale whispered in secret about these things is that we men are in a sort of custody, and a man must not release himself or run away . . . , and that we men are one of the gods' possessions"** (62ab).

Without clear knowledge or evidence, many pious ancients felt this instinctively. Only Jews and Christians had a clear command and a clear reason for it: that man was created by God, in his image, and that God was the God of life who commanded his children to "choose life".

9. Cebes is not satisfied and demands of Socrates reasons—not for the wrongness of suicide, but for Socrates' hope that death can be a good thing, that there is life after death, that the soul is immortal (62cd).

Socrates is not upset but pleased by this wisdom-loving questioning of Cebes (62e), and in the long central section of the *Phaedo* that is omitted here, he gives five arguments for immortality.

Two are negative, answers to arguments against immortality by Cebes and Simmias, based on false analogies between the soul and material things:

a. The soul is not like the invisible harmony produced by a visible lyre (the body), for it is not an effect of the body. If it were, it would perish when the body did.

b. The soul does not die even after it wears out many bodies after cycles of reincarnation [many Greeks believed in reincarnation; in the *Meno* Socrates calls it "a likely story"], as a weaver dies after he outlasts many of the coats he weaves. This analogy, too, is inaccurate.

The three positive arguments Socrates then offers for immortality are ingenious. They are virtually the first purely rational arguments ever invented for immortality. But most philosophers today find them inconclusive.

c. We observe that all things in nature come from their opposites: day from night, night from day, cold from hot, hot from cold, and so on. By this law, not only does death come from life (as we see), but life also comes from death (though this is unseen).

d. If the soul outlasts bodies in the past, by reincarnation, it can do the same in the future. If it is immortal "backwards", it can be immortal "forwards".

Socrates adds a reason for believing in reincarnation by mentioning one of his few positive teachings, developed in the *Meno*, that learning is really remembering, *re*-cognizing, an "aha!" experience like *déjà vu*, which implies a past life before birth.

e. The most abstract and difficult of the arguments (but the most important one) is that the soul, unlike the body, does not *have* life but *is* life; therefore it cannot lose it, anymore than anything can lose its own essence. Bodies get life from their souls; when a soul (life) leaves, the body dies. A soul is a "form" or essence; a body is matter.

Another argument for immortality occurs in the *Republic*, book 10 (608c–611a). It is basically that the most serious body-evils (diseases) kill bodies, but even the worst soul-evils (vices) do not kill souls. This is probably Plato's invention, not Socrates'. The *Republic* marks the probable dividing point between the earlier dialogues, in which Plato is remembering the historical Socrates, and the later dialogues, in which he uses a fictional Socrates as the mouthpiece for his own ideas.

The truth or falsity of religious beliefs, such as life after death, the Greek gods, and reincarnation, is for most people, both believers and nonbelievers, an object of faith rather than rational argument. One of the main functions of philosophy as practiced by Socrates is a critique of religion, finding reasons for (or against) faith. These reasons often claim only probability rather than certainty; and even when they claim certainty, they may be mistaken (for man is not

God and is fallible); but it is surely a gain to use binocular vision, reason *and* faith, and to make at least somewhat clearer and/or more reasonable the ideas most people find the most important in their lives.

By the way, Socrates thought reason could *prove* life after death, *disprove* the Greek gods, and show reincarnation to be "likely" (probable).

He could be wrong. "Who's to say?" There is a very clear answer to that question: You are. Your mind is your own, and it is your own responsibility to "make up your mind". It is also your responsibility to seek reasons for believing or not believing; for the alternatives to reason—prejudices, passions, fashions, fears—do not come *from* you but come *to* you, that is, to your mind, from darker places.

10. After giving what he thinks are three good *reasons* to prove the *existence* of life after death, Socrates gives what he thinks is a good *myth*, or sacred story, to show, symbolically rather than literally, what he thinks is likely to be the *nature* of the next life. (This section is also omitted here.) The essential feature in all his symbols is justice. Injustice has forced him to leave the world of men; he hopes the world of gods is one of perfect justice. (The official stories of the Greek gods, in Homer and Hesiod, picture them as no more just than men are.)

But it is only a guess, as contrasted with the clarity and certainty of the immortality of the soul and its consequence: "**No sensible man would think it proper to rely on things of this kind being just as I have described; but that, since the soul is clearly immortal, this or something like this at any rate is what happens in regard to our souls** and their habitations—that this is so seems to me proper and worthy of the risk of believing; for the risk is noble" (114d).

Socrates' faith is not a guarantee, but a "noble risk", a "leap". But it is not "a leap in the dark"; it is a leap in the light.

11. When someone we love dies, one of the hardest things to endure is our own powerlessness to help him anymore. Thus Socrates' friend Crito asks, as we all do to the dying, "What could we do for you to gratify you most?" And Socrates replies, "What I always say, Criton, nothing very new: Take good care of yourselves" (115b).

But this is not the cliché it seems to be. By "yourselves" Socrates means "your souls", and by "care" he means cultivation of wisdom and virtue. Socrates the altruist is made happy by the attainment of happiness (true happiness, not apparent happiness) by those he loves; and true happiness is the health and perfection of the true self, the soul, not the satisfaction of the desires of the body, which we share with the animals. Socrates' whole philosophy is hidden in the apparent cliché "take care of yourselves."

12. This is as good a place as any to address one of the major objections we are likely to have against this Socratic answer to "know thyself" as being simply the soul, and his ignoring (not an *ignorance*, but a knowing, deliberate *ignoring*) of the body. Elsewhere he even calls the body (*soma* in Greek) the tomb (*sēma*) or prison of the soul, and death consequently a liberation. His hoped-for life after death seems one more appropriate for angels than for men: "Those who have purified themselves enough by philosophy live without bodies altogether forever

after, and come into dwellings even more beautiful . . . , which it is not easy to describe" (114c).

On the one hand, identifying "self" with "soul" rather than body seems right. If your soul were somehow transferred to another's body, and his soul into your body, you would say "I" of your soul even though it was in his body, rather than of your body, which was now hosting the life and consciousness (soul) of the other. This identification of self with soul is a necessary corrective to our habitual materialism, and it produces a light, noble detachment: when his friends ask, **"How are we to bury you?"** Socrates pokes fun at their implied materialism, which identifies Socrates with his corpse:

"How you like," said he, "if you catch me and I don't escape you." At the same time, laughing gently and looking towards us, he said, "Criton doesn't believe me, my friends, that this is I, Socrates, now talking with you and laying down each of my injunctions, but he thinks me to be what he will see shortly, a corpse, and asks, if you please, how to bury me! I have been saying all this long time, that when I have drunk the potion, I shall not be here then with you; I shall have gone clear away to some bliss of the blest, as they call it. But he thinks I am talking nonsense, just to console myself, yes and you too." (115cd)

Yes, I am not a body that temporarily has a soul (its life) and will soon lose it and become a corpse; I am a soul that temporarily has a body and will soon lose it. At death I will lose my body, not my soul!

And the consequences of this insight are ennobling and liberating.

But, on the other hand, there are many good reasons for saying a qualified No to Socrates after saying a qualified Yes. I say, "Two cheers for Socrates' teaching" here, not three; for

a. My body is not just an object but an aspect of myself *as subject* of consciousness. In fact, we are sometimes *surprised* to discover that it is also an object, for instance, when we reach out in the dark for a friend's hand and touch our own by mistake: "That thing out there—that's *me!*"

b. If we believe God designed and created us with bodies and that God makes no mistakes and that he also created angels (spirits without bodies), it follows that we are not angels in disguise, nor do we have bodies by mistake or accident.

c. Do we really prefer Socrates' picture of a bodiless life after death to one with perfection of body as well as soul?

d. Socrates does not do justice to the importance and goodness of the body. It is not a tomb or a prison. It helps the soul to attain wisdom by delivering data to it via the senses. It procreates more human beings, the greatest things in the known universe. It expresses the soul's thoughts and volitions, like an artist's medium.

e. Socrates does not do justice to the *relationship* between soul and body, the "psychosomatic unity", which is more like the relation between the "matter" and the "form" or essence of a work of art (for instance, the syllables and the meaning of a play) than it is like the relation between a prisoner and a cage, or a rider and a horse, or a ghost and a machine, or an angel and a beast.

If these criticisms are valid, some serious consequences follow:

a. There is no reincarnation. The essential meaning of *Hamlet* cannot be reincarnated in the syllables of *Macbeth*. My body is not one of many external instruments, prisons, houses, or tombs, but a dimension of the unique me, therefore uniquely mine.

b. Socrates has not wholly succeeded in his quest to obey the god's first law, "know thyself". His discovery of the soul is the essential *beginning*, as is his Lesson One about wisdom, but not the end.

c. Socrates' last and most precious conviction, that evil men cannot harm good men, must be modified: If they can harm my body, and my body is a part of me, then they *can* harm me. The psychosomatic unity also entails the conclusion that they can harm my soul indirectly, through my body. For example, they can deprive me of knowledge, and they can at least make virtue much *harder* for me to practice by their ill treatment. It is difficult to be peaceful and charitable when one is being tortured.

And yet—surely the truth about the primacy of the soul, which Socrates taught, is more important than the truth about the importance of the body, which he failed to teach. A materialist denies the first, a spiritualist the second. If they are both wrong, as most people believe, they must be dealt with and refuted by reason, ideally in dialogue, ideally Socratic dialogue. (An ingenious but tricky and difficult attempt to do just that, and to justify Socrates' "spiritualism" by going beyond it to the denial of the very reality of matter, is George Berkeley's *Three Dialogues between Hylas and Philonous.*)

13. Socrates lives his philosophy. He practices what he preaches to the end. Thus he does not delay and drinks the poison **"quite cheerfully, Echecrates, not a tremble, not a change in colour or looks"** (117b), while all around him break down weeping.

His piety persists to the end, too, as he asks the jailer whether he may pour out some of the potion as a libation to "someone". (He may not, so he offers a prayer instead.) And this is the man who is guilty of atheism?

Taking the poison was *not* suicide. (The "Hemlock Society", which advocates suicide, misuses the name of Socrates' famous poison.) It was the penalty imposed on him, not *his* will and choice. In fact, just a few minutes earlier he had tried to prove to his disciples that suicide is wrong and impious (point 8). His only choice is the *manner* of dying: dignified or undignified, calm or kicking and screaming. If Socrates committed suicide simply because he did not use violence against his killers, then so did Jesus.

A martyr is not a suicide. In fact, a martyr is the opposite of a suicide. A martyr loves something so much that he will give up everything else for it, even his life, if required to. A suicide loves nothing in life enough to live for it, even though piety requires him to live (if Socrates is right) and nothing requires him to die.

14. Socrates' humor also persists to the end. His very last words are a joke. (Martyrs often do that, as if playing with life as a toy: St. Lawrence, roasted to

death on a barbecue spit, said "Turn me over, please; I'm not quite done yet on the other side.")

Socrates' last words are: **"Criton, we owe a cock to Asclepios; pay it without fail"** (118a).

Asclepios was the Greek god of healing. Pious Greeks slept in his temples, hoping for a cure. Some Greek doctors claimed to be descended from him (Greek gods sometimes mated with mortals); many claimed to be inspired by him. When a pious Greek was healed of a serious, life-threatening disease, he would pay not only his human doctor but also the god Asclepios, who supposedly inspired his doctor. A sheep was a rich man's offering, a cock was a poor man's.

But Socrates was never sick, as far as any records mention. So why does he offer the gift of thanksgiving for a cure from a life-threatening illness?

The "cure" he is receiving is death. The illness is life. This illness is universal and fatal: nobody gets out of here alive. Socrates sees life in this world and this body as an illness that only a god can cure.

15. Plato's concluding epitaph for Socrates is as simple, short, clear, and direct as Socrates himself: **"This was the end of our comrade, Echecrates, a man, as we would say, of all then living we had ever met, the noblest and the wisest and most just"** (118a).

Plato is a good strategist: he keeps his trump card till the end. The *Phaedo*, as we have seen, is divided into two parts: Socrates' words to prove immortality, and his deeds (point 3, p. 133). Plato knows that the most convincing proof of Socrates' belief is its effect on his life, especially at his life's most critical moment, his confrontation with death. In the words of an old cliché, "What you are speaks so loud I can hardly hear what you say." Socrates' arguments for immortality (which we merely summarized) are not his strongest legacy; he himself is. For when the idea of Socrates and the idea of death meet here, it is the idea of death that is changed.

And your life, too.

Acknowledgments

The author and publisher express their appreciation to Penguin Putnam Inc. New York, for permission to reprint excerpts from *The Apology* and *Phaedo* from *The Great Dialogues of Plato*, by Plato, translated by W. H. D. Rouse. Copyright © 1956, renewed © 1984 by J. C. G. Rouse. Used by permission of Dutton Signet, a division of Penguin Putnam Inc.

Selections from *Euthyphro* are excerpted from Lane Cooper's translation in *On the Trial and the Death of Socrates* (Ithaca, N.Y., © 1941) as included in *The Collected Dialogues of Plato*, Edith Hamilton and Huntington Cairns, eds. (Princeton, N.J.: Princeton University Press, © 1961, renewed 1989). Reprinted by permission of Princeton University Press.